Defective 1st printing of
this reprint

(pp 10-19 in 1st & 3rd
papers are all present, but
alternate)

HEWITSON
ON
BUTTERFLIES
1867-1877

With a Preface by
Dr. L. G. Higgins

HAMPTON
1972
E. W. CLASSEY LTD.

HEWITSON ON BUTTERFLIES
With a Preface by Dr. L. G. Higgins

E. W. CLASSEY LTD.
353 Hanworth Road, Hampton, Middlesex
England

Distributed in U.S.A.
by
ENTOMOLOGICAL REPRINT SPECIALISTS
P.O. Box 77971, Dockweiler Station
Los Angeles, California 90007

ISBN 0 900848 56 1

Printed by Biddles Ltd., Guildford, Surrey

HEWITSON ON BUTTERFLIES
With a Preface by Dr. L. G. Higgins

Descriptions of one hundred new species of Hesperidae
1st part April 20th 1867 (pp. ii; 1–25)
2nd part March 23rd 1868 (pp. 25–56)

Descriptions of some new species of Lycaenidae
1 part June 1st 1868 (pp. 1–36)

Equatorial Lepidoptera collected by Mr. Buckley
1st part December 2nd 1869 (pp. ii; 1–16)
2nd part December 15th 1869 (pp. 17–32)
3rd part December 30th 1869 (pp. 33–48)
4th part March 10th 1870 (pp. 49–80 and Index)
5th part April 11th 1877 (pp. 81–96)

Bolivian Butterflies collected by Mr. Buckley
1 part November 1st 1874 (pp. 1–22)

PREFACE

by Dr. L. G. Higgins

WILLIAM CHAPMAN HEWITSON was one of the best known and most respected of British Entomologists in the middle years of the last century. He became a surveyor by profession and according to contemporary biographers, his interest in natural history dated from boyhood. He must have given much attention to the study and collection of butterflies, and at the same time, he was an accomplished artist, like his contemporaries J. O. Westwood and A. G. Butler. No doubt it was partly on this account that, at the age of 40, he became associated with Edward Doubleday in producing the "Genera of Diurnal Lepidoptera" (1846 and later), an original and classic work of great importance. Figures for the 86 coloured plates in this book were all drawn by Hewitson, and the later plates also lithographed by him ("del. et lith."). Indeed, Hewitson was his own artist for every one of the hundreds of figures he published later. In his middle age, now a rich man, Hewitson continued seriously to build up an important collection of butterflies, using every possible means, including financial support to exploratory expeditions, purchase of specimens, etc. It was a time of discovery, and from Central and South America especially the stream of undescribed species became embarrassing. Hewitson dealt with these as well as he could in his second important work—"Illustrations of . . . Exotic Butterflies"—which began to appear in 1852, issued in quarterly parts and continued for 20 years. Hewitson alone was responsible for every figure. He realized rightly the importance of figures and the frequent difficulty or impossibility of identification of butterflies by written descriptions alone. In his Preface to the booklet "Descriptions of 100 Hesperidae" referred to below, he begins with the following sentence—"I would apologise for adding to the load of useless entomological literature which is now so rapidly accumulating by attempting to describe a group of butterflies, to elucidate which, descriptions alone are utterly inadequate, were it not that I hope to figure all of them in the 'Exotic Butterflies'!" This intention was not carried out completely. In 1863 Hewitson commenced the production of another major work—"Illustrations of Diurnal Lepidoptera"—concerned exclusively with his favourite group, the Lycaenidae. This was a period of great activity which continued almost until his death in 1878. In the years 1864–1877 Hewitson made no fewer than 75 contributions to various entomological periodicals and learned societies, in addition to continued production of his major works.

In view of Hewitson's high reputation and his association with lepidopterists in many countries, it is strange that his four small descriptive pamphlets, included in the present volume, are among the rarities of modern entomological literature. Two were not available to the authors of the Index Litteraturae Entomologicae and are recorded in Vol. 2 as unseen (Descriptions of . . . Lycaenidae 1868 and Descriptions of . . . Hesperidae 1867). A fourth pamphlet is not recorded (Bolivian Butterflies 1874). These little books, in small octavo form, were all privately published, evidently in very small editions, and they are truly important contributions. They include the first descriptions of 10 valid genera and 403 butterfly species, almost all from Central and South America, mostly taken from Hewitson's own extensive collections, but not rarely of specimens provided by H. W. Bates, W. W. Saunders, Salvin and Godman, and more rarely sent by Boisduval and Semper. The descriptive text for each species usually occupies about half a page, including a record of provenance, etc., but lacking coloured figures. For many species figures were provided in the last two volumes of the Illustrations of Exotic Butterflies, but about 203 species were never figured by Hewitson. Later identification of many of these might have been extremely difficult, but fortunately Hewitson's entire collection passed to the British Museum after his death and the original specimens have been carefully preserved there in the Type Collection. In fact all the species named in these pamphlets were identified and recorded by W. F. Kirby in his catalogue of 1871–77, and in later years by Röber, Fruhstorfer and others in Seitz, Vol. 5, etc. The titles and contents of the four pamphlets are as follows:—

"Descriptions of one hundred new species of Hesperidae." 1st part April 20th, 1867; 2nd part March 23rd, 1868. Included the genera *Aethilla, Caecina, Hesperilla* and 100 species, 52 of which not figured by Hewitson.

"Descriptions of some new species of Lycaenidae". 1 part June 1st, 1868. Included 76 species, 4 of which figures in "Ill. Diurnal Lep."

"Equatorial Lepidoptera collected by Mr. Buckley."* 1st part December 2nd 1869; 2nd part December 15th, 1869; 3rd part December 30th 1869; 4th part March 10th, 1870; 5th part April 11th, 1877. Includes genera *Lucilla, Imelda, Compsoteria, Threnodes, Zabirnia* and 175 species, of which 92 are not figured by Hewitson.

"Bolivian Butterflies collected by Mr. Buckley." 1 part 1874. Includes genera *Hermathena*, *Xynias* and 52 species reported or described. 15 species not figured by Hewitson.

It is probable that these booklets were rapidly produced and published in order to establish priority of nomenclature, perhaps in very restricted editions, for dispersal to Hewitson's entomological colleagues, and personal friends. There is no note on the paper covers of any sale price. It is not known whether the books were ever offered for sale, but they were accepted as valid publications by the authors mentioned above and even more recently by A. F. Hemming in his last work—"Generic Names of Butterflies" (1967).

*No title page published.

DESCRIPTIONS

OF

ONE HUNDRED NEW SPECIES

OF

HESPERIDÆ.

BY

W. C. HEWITSON.

PART I.

LONDON:

JOHN VAN VOORST, 1 PATERNOSTER ROW.

April 20th, 1867.

PREFACE.

I WOULD apologize for adding to the load of useless entomological literature which is now so rapidly accumulating by attempting to describe a group of butterflies, to elucidate which descriptions alone are utterly inadequate, were it not that I hope to figure all of them in the 'Exotic Butterflies.'

Dr. Gray, who was about to have the *Hesperidæ* of the British Museum catalogued and described, generously relinquished his intention upon my stating to him what I have said above, and promising him that I would undertake to figure them; and it is that I may keep my promise that I now issue (to appropriate the species) what I consider when unaided by figures more than worthless.

When we have 150 species which, except in form and size, have scarcely any trait on the upperside by which to distinguish them from each other, and all possess the transparent spots in common, it is by a very faithful figure alone that they can be satisfactorily separated. I have always felt, and have acted accordingly, that I should by descriptions only receive the anathema of future entomologists, whilst by a fair figure I might be entitled to their benediction. Such have been my own sensations when I have puzzled over a vague description in vain, or have at once been able, by such figures as those of Guyer and Herrich-Schäffer, to recognize my species. The specific characters of the *Hesperidæ* are usually most conspicuous in the colouring of the underside of the posterior wing. I hope that the *Hesperidæ* may complete a fifth volume of the 'Exotic Butterflies' and form a complete monograph, should I have species sufficient to fill a fourth volume without them and health to figure them.

HESPERIDÆ.

Genus ERYCIDES.

1. Erycides Phoronis.

Alis rufis: anticis maculis tribus vitreis nigro marginatis: posticis
productis, dentatis, macula vitrea fasciisque fuscis: infra ad
basin flavis.

UPPERSIDE rufous. Anterior wing with three transparent spots bordered with black: one near the middle large
and trifid, one outside of this bifid, and one before the apex
trifid: the nervures black. Posterior wing angular, dentated:
crossed by two bands of dark brown.

UNDERSIDE. Both wings rufous, with the basal half
yellow, bordered outwardly with black, and crossed on the
posterior wing by two black bands, and outside of these by
a broken band as above.

Exp. 2 inches. *Hab.* New Granada.
In the collection of W. C. Hewitson.

A beautiful species, near to *H. Santhilarius* of Latreille.

2. Erycides Amystis.

Alis aurantiaco-flavis: anticis maculis quinque (una in medio tripartita) vitreis nigro marginatis: posticis dentatis, macula vitrea
fasciaque angulata nigra: infra flavis.

UPPERSIDE rufous-orange. Anterior wing with five
transparent spots bordered with black: one near the middle

trifid, one outside of this bifid, two small ones between the last and the spot near the apex, which is bifid: the outer margin rufous. Posterior wing angular, dentated, with one indistinct transparent spot before the middle: crossed at the middle by an indistinct band of brown, and beyond it by a zigzag band of black: the outer margin black.

UNDERSIDE as above, except that it is orange-yellow, that the transparent spots are not bordered with brown, and that the posterior wing has two spots of brown near the base.

Exp. 1$\frac{8}{10}$ inch. *Hab.* New Granada.

In the collection of W. C. Hewitson.

Closely allied to *P. nobilis* of Cramer.

3. Erycides Araxes.

Alis fuscis fimbria nivea: anticis maculis decem vitreis, tribus in fascia positis: posticis infra fasciis duabus flavis.

UPPERSIDE dark brown, the fringe snow-white, intersected with dark brown. Anterior wing with ten transparent white spots: three forming a central transverse band, three outside of these forming a short oblique band, three before the apex, and the tenth a minute spot at the costal margin.

UNDERSIDE dark brown. Anterior wing as above, except that it is rufous at the base. Posterior wing with the base and inner margin and two transverse bands orange-yellow. The first band before the middle, regular and trifid; the outer band beyond the middle curved outwards, undulated and composed of several spots.

Exp. 2 inches. *Hab.* Mexico.

In the Collection of W. C. Hewitson.

Like species of *Eudamus* in general appearance, but with the antennæ of this genus.

Genus EUDAMUS, *Swainson*.

GONIURUS, *Westwood*.

1. Eudamus Alcæus.

Alis fuscis: anticis maculis decem vitreis, quatuor in fascia positis: posticis infra cinereis, macula ad basin, fascia maculisque tribus minutis nigris et fascia lata alba.

UPPERSIDE dark brown, covered near the base with ochreous hair: the fringe black and white alternately. Anterior wing with ten pale yellow transparent spots: four in a band at the centre, one square outside of these, one oblique and linear, and four in a band before the apex. Posterior wing with a long tail.

UNDERSIDE lilac-grey clouded on the anterior wing with brown. Anterior wing with the spots as above. Posterior wing with nine black spots: two near the base, three in a central band, and four beyond the middle, three of which are small, placed in the form of a triangle and followed by a broad band of white.

Exp. $2\frac{2}{10}$ inches. *Hab.* Nicaragua.

In the Collection of W. C. Hewitson.

2. Eudamus albofasciatus.

Alis fuscis: anticis maculis vitreis: his infra macula triangulari apicali: posticis fascia alba: cauda longissima.

UPPERSIDE dark brown. Anterior wing with eight transparent spots: four forming a central band (the lowest spot very minute), one outside of these, and three in a band before the apex. Posterior wing with a very long tail.

UNDERSIDE. Anterior wing as above, except that it is grey near the apex and marked by a triangular dark brown spot. Posterior wing dark brown, crossed obliquely by a central band of white : a submarginal band of grey.

Exp. 2 inches. *Hab.* Guatemala (Polochic Valley).

In the Collection of W. C. Hewitson, kindly presented by Mr. Salvin.

3. Eudamus Aminias.

Alis fuscis : anticis maculis decem vitreis, quatuor in fascia positis : posticis infra macula ad basin, fasciis duabus, macula minuta (flavo punctata) margineque fuscis.

UPPERSIDE dark rufous-brown : the fringe black and white alternately. Anterior wing with ten pale yellow transparent spots : four in a central broken band, two (one minute) outside of these, and four before the apex. Posterior wing with a long tail.

UNDERSIDE rufous-brown. Anterior wing as above, except that it is clouded with darker brown. Posterior wing with three dark brown spots at the base : crossed by two irregular broken bands of dark brown, followed by a small brown spot bordered above with pale yellow : a broad submarginal band of dark brown.

Exp. $1\frac{8}{10}$ inch. *Hab.* Minas Geraes.

In the Collection of W. C. Hewitson.

4. Eudamus undulatus.

Alis fuscis : anticis maculis vitreis : anticis infra macula apicali fusca : posticis fusco undulatis, basi fasciisque duabus fuscis.

UPPERSIDE ochreous-brown : the fringe pale yellow : on the anterior wing brown and white alternately, on the posterior wing broad and spotted with brown. Anterior wing with nine transparent pale yellow spots : four (the first minute) forming a central band, one outside of these, and four before the apex. Posterior wing with long broad tails.

UNDERSIDE. Anterior wing as above, except that it is paler and grey near the apex marked by a large dark brown spot. Posterior wing pale grey-brown, undulated throughout with brown and clouded, except near the outer margin, with large undefined brown spots : tinted with lilac in the centre.

Exp. $1\frac{9}{10}$ inch.

In the Collection of W. C. Hewitson.

5. Eudamus Amisus.

Alis rufo-fuscis: anticis maculis novem vitreis, quatuor in fascia positis: posticis margine exteriori reflexo: his infra macula at basin nigra fasciisque duabus fuscis.

UPPERSIDE rufous-brown. Anterior wing with nine pale yellow transparent spots : four (the first bifid) forming a central band, two (one minute) outside of these, and three before the apex. Posterior wing tailed: the outer margin rounded.

UNDERSIDE. Anterior wing as above. Posterior wing lilac-brown with a round black spot near the base : crossed by two bands of dark brown and a submarginal band of brown broken into spots from the apex to the middle.

Exp. $1\frac{7}{10}$ inch.

In the Collection of W. C. Hewitson.

Easily distinguished by the rounded margin of the posterior wing.

6. Eudamus Asine.

Alis rufo-fuscis: anticis maculis octo vitreis, quatuor (una minutissima) in medio positis, maculisque duabus fuscis: posticis macula fasciaque fuscis.

UPPERSIDE rufous-brown : the fringe (except near the apex of the anterior wing) pale yellow. Anterior wing with eight transparent white spots : four in the middle (the first minute, the other three placed in the form of a triangle) and four (the first very minute) before the apex : two brown spots

Exp. $\frac{9}{10}$ inch. *Hab.* Ecuador.

In the Collection of W. C. Hewitson.

A variable species. In some specimens the blue on the posterior wing is confined to the marginal lunular spots.

13. Thecla Opalia.

UPPERSIDE. *Male.*—Dark brown : the base of the anterior wing below the middle and the whole of the posterior wing (with the exception of the apex and outer margin, which are brown) cerulean blue. Anterior wing with the discal spot pale rufous-brown.

UNDERSIDE rufous-brown, tinted with lilac. Both wings crossed by a band of white spots, bordered inwardly with dark brown : posterior wing with one tail : a submarginal band of brown spots, bordered inwardly with white : the lobe dark brown : the space near it white, irrorated with brown : a submarginal white line above the tail.

Exp. 1 inch. *Hab.* Amazon.

In the Collection of H. W. Bates and W. W. Saunders.

14. Thecla Ophia.

UPPERSIDE. *Male.*—Dark brown. The base and inner margin to the middle of the anterior wing and the posterior wing (except the inner and costal margins, which are brown) green-blue. Anterior wing with the discal spot dark brown, unusually large and oval.

UNDERSIDE pale rufous-grey, or stone-colour *. Both wings crossed below the middle by a band of black, bordered outwardly with white and inwardly on the posterior wing with orange. Anterior wing with a short band at the anal angle. Posterior wing with two tails : a spot between them and the lobe black, crowned with orange : a submarginal line of white.

Exp. 1 inch. *Hab.* Amazon.

In the Collection of H. W. Bates.

---

* This colour, so prevalent in this group of Butterflies, would perhaps be best described as drab.

15. Thecla ornea.

UPPERSIDE. *Female.*—Dark brown: the fringe dull white.

UNDERSIDE rufous, pale. Both wings crossed beyond the middle by a band of dark brown bordered inwardly with scarlet, outwardly with white: commencing on the costal margin of the posterior wing in a round spot: both with an indistinct submarginal brown band, bordered outwardly with indistinct white: both with the outer margin black. Posterior wing with two tails: the anal angle and a large spot between the tails (which is marked by a minute black spot) scarlet: the lobe black: a submarginal line of white.

Exp. $\frac{9}{10}$ inch. *Hab.* Amazon.

In the Collection of H. W. Bates.

16. Thecla Halala.

UPPERSIDE. *Male.*—Dull grey-blue. Anterior wing with the costal and the outer margin (which is broad at the apex) dark brown. Posterior wing with one tail: the outer margin dark brown, narrow.

UNDERSIDE pale rufous-grey, or stone-colour. Anterior wing crossed beyond the middle by a band of indistinct minute brown spots bordered outwardly with white. Posterior wing crossed at the middle by a distinct broken band of white bordered inwardly with black: a submarginal band of brown broken into spots near the apex, and bordered on both sides with white: the lobe and the spot at the base of the tail black, broadly bordered above with scarlet: a submarginal line of white: the outer margin black.

Exp. $1\frac{3}{20}$ inch. *Hab.* Amazon.

In the Collection of W. W. Saunders and H. W. Bates.

17. Thecla Hyccara.

UPPERSIDE. *Male.*—Dark brown: the inner margin of the posterior wing from the base to beyond the middle, and the whole of the posterior wing, except the costal and outer band near the middle, two large spots near the inner margin (the lowest bordered with white), and the anal lobe black.

Exp. 1½ inch. *Hab.* Rio de Janeiro.

In the Collection of W. C. Hewitson.

11. Eudamus Athesis.

Alis fuscis: anticis maculis decem indistinctis vitreis: infra flavo irroratis: anticis macula fasciaque submarginali ochraceis: posticis macula fasciisque duabus rufo-fuscis nigro marginatis.

UPPERSIDE dark brown. Anterior wing with ten very indistinct transparent spots : four (the first bifid, the fourth minute) in a narrow broken central band, two outside of these, and four before the apex. Posterior wing with a short broad tail.

UNDERSIDE rufous brown : the apical half of the anterior wing and the whole of the posterior wing irrorated throughout with yellow. Anterior wing dark brown outside the band : a spot near the apex and a submarginal band of small spots brown. Posterior wing with a spot at the base, two transverse bands (the outer band bordered on both sides with zigzag black lines), and a submarginal band all brown.

Exp. 1$\frac{8}{10}$ inch. *Hab.* Venezuela.

In the Collection of W. C. Hewitson.

GONILOBA, *Westwood.*

12. Eudamus Antæus.

Alis rufo-fuscis: anticis maculis flavis vitreis: his infra fascia submarginali cinerea : posticis fascia centrali argenteo-alba.

UPPERSIDE dark rufous brown, thickly covered with ochreous hair near the body. Anterior wing with eight transparent dull yellow spots : four (three of which are large) in a central band, one outside of these, and three (minute) before the apex. Posterior wing with a broad lobe at the anal angle.

UNDERSIDE dark rufous-brown. Anterior wing as above, except that there is a broad submarginal band of lilac-grey. Posterior wing with a minute white spot near the base: crossed at the middle by a silvery band of white, narrow at the costal margin, broad below: irrorated with grey near the outer margin.

Exp. $2\frac{3}{10}$ inch.

In the Collection of W. C. Hewitson.

Very near to *E. Clarus*, from which it differs in the form of the silvery white band.

13. Eudamus Asander.

Alis fuscis: anticis maculis vitreis: anticis infra margine exteriori cinereo irrorato: posticis fascia lata centrali alba (puncto fusco notata) late cinereo marginata.

UPPERSIDE dark brown thickly covered with ochreous hair. Anterior wing with eight transparent pale yellow spots: four of equal size in an oblique straight central band, one outside of these, and three minute (two together and one far apart) before the apex. Posterior wing lobed.

UNDERSIDE. Anterior wing as above except that the outer margin is broadly grey. Posterior wing crossed by a central broad band of white marked by a small brown spot and dentated outwardly, where it is bordered with grey, which extends to the outer margin.

Exp. $2\frac{3}{10}$ inches. *Hab.* Amazon (Ega).

In the Collection of W. C. Hewitson.

Near to *E. Exadeus*. Varies considerably, some examples having the central white band on the underside of the posterior wing narrow, nearly resembling the next species.

14. Eudamus Aurunce.

Alis fuscis: anticis maculis novem vitreis, quatuor in fascia, quatuor prope apicem valde oblique positis: posticis infra fascia angusta alba.

22. Thecla Laconia.

UPPERSIDE. *Female.*—Grey-brown, darker towards the outer margins. Posterior wing with two tails ; a line of white at the base of the tails : the fringe grey-white.

UNDERSIDE pale stone-colour. Both wings crossed by a band of white, bordered inwardly with dark brown : both with a submarginal band of brown (bordered on both sides with white), indistinct and pale on the anterior wing, dark and zigzag on the posterior wing. Posterior wing with the lobe and the spot between the tails black, broadly bordered above with orange : a submarginal line of white : the margin black.

Exp. $\frac{19}{20}$ inch. *Hab.* Amazon.

In the Collection of H. W. Bates.

23. Thecla Gedrosia.

UPPERSIDE. *Male.*—Dark brown. Anterior wing with the base of the inner margin blue. Posterior wing with two tails, dull blue from the base to the middle : the lobe orange.

UNDERSIDE rufous-brown. Both wings crossed beyond the middle by a brown band : indistinct on the anterior wing. Posterior wing with the lobe black, bordered above by a minute spot of white and a large spot of scarlet : the black spot between the tails broadly bordered above with scarlet, and below and outside of it with white : the space between the spots white.

Exp. $1\frac{3}{10}$ inch. *Hab.* Amazon (Tapajos).

In the Collection of H. W. Bates.

24. Thecla Lemuria.

UPPERSIDE brilliant morpho-blue. Anterior wing with the costal and outer margin and apex broadly brown : the discal spot beyond the middle, large, oval, dark brown.

UNDERSIDE pale stone-colour. Both wings crossed beyond the middle by a band of brown, bordered outwardly with white, and inwardly with orange-yellow : commencing on the costal margin of the posterior wing by an isolated spot, with the W strongly marked near the anal angle : both wings with a very indistinct submarginal band. Posterior wing with the lobe black, crowned first with white, and above that with orange: a large orange spot between the tails marked by a small black spot : the space between the spots white irrorated with black and crowned with orange and black.

Exp. $\frac{17}{20}$ inch. *Hab.* Amazon.

In the Collection of H. W. Bates.

25. Thecla Orcynia.

UPPERSIDE dark brown. Anterior wing with the basal half nearly (except the costal margin) brilliant blue. Posterior wing (except the base and margins, which are rufous-brown) brilliant blue : the outer margin dark brown.

UNDERSIDE pale stone-colour. Both wings crossed beyond the middle by a band of white, slightly bordered inwardly with brown. Anterior wing with a submarginal band of white. Posterior wing with one tail and three submarginal white bands : the lobe and the spot at the base of the tails black, bordered above with scarlet and yellow.

Exp. $1\frac{7}{20}$ inch. *Hab.* Guatemala (Polochic valley).

In the Collection of Messrs. Salvin and Godman.

26. Thecla Bactriana.

UPPERSIDE. *Male.*—Dark brown. The base and inner margin of the anterior wing and the whole of the posterior wing (except the costal margin, which is rufous-brown) blue. Anterior wing with the discal spot before the middle, large, oval, and red-brown.

UNDERSIDE pale ochreous. Anterior wing with the costal half (which is marked by a linear spot at the base, a trifid spot at the middle, and two small white spots near the apex) dark brown. Posterior wing with two tails; a

UPPERSIDE rufous-brown. Anterior wing with seven pale yellow spots : four forming a central band, one outside of these, and two (very minute) before the apex. Posterior wing slightly lobed.

UNDERSIDE rufous. The apical half of the anterior wing and the whole of the posterior wing irrorated with grey. Both wings crossed near the middle by two lines of rufous brown. Posterior wing crossed by a third line nearer the base.

Exp. 2 inches. *Hab.* South America.

In the Collection of W. C. Hewitson.

19. Eudamus Elaites.

Alis rufo-fuscis : anticis maculis decem vitreis : infra rufis, ad basin flavis : posticis macula nigra prope basin : fasciis duabus transversis rufo-brunneis.

UPPERSIDE dark brown. Anterior wing with ten transparent white spots : four forming a central band, three (minute) outside of these, the last nearly touching the three minute spots near the apex. Posterior wing slightly lobed.

UNDERSIDE rufous : the base of both wings ochreous : the fringe broad, grey spotted with brown. Anterior wing with the central band broader : a submarginal line of brown. Posterior wing with a black spot near the base, crossed by two broad irregular bands of dark rufous brown followed by a third band of indistinct rufous spots.

Exp. 1½ inch. *Hab.* Minas Geraes.

In the Collection of W. C. Hewitson.

20. Eudamus Eriopis.

Alis rufo-fuscis : anticis maculis parvis vitreis : posticis fascia maculari fusca : his infra maculis novem ochraceis.

UPPERSIDE rufous-brown. Anterior wing with eight minute transparent white spots : three (apart) in a line at the middle, two outside of these, and three before the apex. Posterior wing crossed from the costal margin to the middle by a band of dark brown spots.

UNDERSIDE as above, except that the posterior wing has a band of ochreous spots in place of the brown spots of the upperside, and four other spots of the same colour—two towards the costal margin and two within the cell.

Exp. $2\frac{2}{10}$ inches. *Hab.* Amazon (Tapajos).

In the Collection of W. C. Hewitson.

This and nearly all of the following species have the fine flexible points of the antennæ much longer than in those hitherto described.

21. Eudamus Doriscus.

Myscelus Sebaldus, *Westwood in Doubleday and Hewitson's Genera of Diurn. Lepid.* pl. 78. f. 6.

This is certainly not the *Sebaldus Crameri* of Latreille of Cramer's figures, plate 342. A, B.

22. Eudamus Etias.

Alis rufo-fuscis: anticis maculis septem vitreis: posticis macula fasciaque fuscis obscuris, infra maculis ochraceis.

UPPERSIDE rufous. Anterior wing with seven transparent spots : four in the middle, two of which are large and one lunular, three at the apex (one minute). Posterior wing with a central spot and macular band of obscure brown spots.

UNDERSIDE as above except that the posterior wing has several ochreous spots in place of the brown spots of the upperside : two or three in the centre with others forming a semicircle below them.

Exp. $2\frac{1}{2}$ inches. *Hab.* Amazon.

In the Collection of W. C. Hewitson, from Mr. Bates.

Near to *P. Eurybates,* Cramer, plate 393.

wings crossed beyond the middle by a band of dark brown
bordered outwardly with white : both with a submarginal
band of brown, very indistinct on the anterior wing, bordered
inwardly with white on the posterior wing : the lobe, the spot
between the tails, and half the space between them black,
bordered above with orange.

Exp. 1$\frac{3}{20}$ inch. *Hab.* Mexico.

In the Collection of W. C. Hewitson.

Very like the last described on the underside, but quite
different above.

32. Thecla Beroea.

UPPERSIDE. *Male.*—Grey-brown, the fringe grey-white.
Anterior wing with a dark brown square discal spot within the
cell. Posterior wing with one tail : the lobe orange : the
spot at the base of the tail large, dark brown.

UNDERSIDE pale grey or stone-colour. Both wings with
a white line at the end of the cell : both crossed by a band of
white rufous on its inner border, broadly bordered with white
outwardly, straight and beyond the middle on the anterior
wing, slightly angular and at the middle of the posterior
wing : both with a submarginal band of white spots, lunular
on the posterior wing. Posterior wing with a band of white
before the middle, the lobe and the usual spot black, bordered
above with orange : the space between them brown, irrorated
with white.

Exp. 1$\frac{3}{20}$ *Hab.* Mexico.

In the Collection of W. C. Hewitson.

Near to *T. Daraba,* ' Lycænidæ,' plate 36. fig. 89.

33. Thecla Bassania.

UPPERSIDE. *Male.*—Brilliant blue. Anterior wing with
the costal margin and more than the apical half dark brown.
Posterior wing with two tails : the costal and inner margins
broadly rufous-brown : the outer margin narrow, dark brown.

UNDERSIDE rufous-grey or stone-colour. Both wings with two lines of white at the end of the cell : both crossed by a band bordered on both sides with undulated white lines : both with two submarginal bands of irregular white spots and a line of white. Posterior wing with two undulated lines of white near the base : the lobe and black spot at the anal angle bordered above with orange.

Exp. 1$\frac{3}{10}$ inch. *Hab.* Mexico.

In the Collection of W. C. Hewitson.

34. Thecla Carthæa.

UPPERSIDE. *Male.*—Violet-blue, tinted with green towards the margins. Anterior wing with the apex dark brown. Posterior wing with one tail and three or four spots of gold-green at the anal angle.

UNDERSIDE olive-brown : the nervures black. Anterior wing with three spots of scarlet and three spots of gold-green near the base : a trifid spot of gold-green on the costal margin. Posterior wing with one spot of scarlet and one spot of gold-green at the base : anal angle with six or seven gold-green spots.

Exp. 1$\frac{5}{20}$ inch. *Hab.* Mexico.

In the Collection of W. C. Hewitson.

Near *T. Halesus.*

35. Thecla Carpasia.

UPPERSIDE blue-green : the nervures black. Anterior wing with the outer half dark brown. Posterior wing with two tails : the apex broadly dark brown : the outer margin and anal angle black, marked by a band of silver-green spots.

UNDERSIDE olive-brown, with the nervures of the posterior wing black. Anterior wing with two spots of scarlet and three of silver-green at the base. Posterior wing with the base, the inner margin, and anal angle black, marked by five

UPPERSIDE dark rufous-brown. Anterior wing with the outer margin rounded : six transparent spots : four apart from each other in a curved band at the middle (the lowest spot minute), one outside of these, and one only before the apex. Posterior wing with three minute transparent spots, one of which is central.

UNDERSIDE rufous. Anterior wing as above, except that it has two minute brown spots near the apex. Posterior wing with four white spots between the transparent spots and the inner margin, a brown spot touching the central white spot, and five other brown spots forming a semicircle with four of the white spots.

Exp. $2\frac{11}{20}$ inches. *Hab.* Amazon (Tapajos).

In the Collection of W. C. Hewitson, from Mr. Bates.

28. Eudamus Pelignus.

Alis rufis : anticis margine externo reflexo, maculis quinque parvis vitreis: posticis puncto vitreo punctisque fuscis: his infra macula centrali fasciaque macularum fuscarum albo punctatarum.

UPPERSIDE rufous : the outer margin brown. Anterior wing with the outer margin rounded : five small transparent spots (one bifid) apart from each other, one only before the apex. Posterior wing with one minute transparent spot : a central spot and some minute spots (forming a transverse band with the transparent spot) brown.

UNDERSIDE as above, except that the posterior wing has the brown spots marked indistinctly with white, and three other white spots bordered with brown between the transparent spot and the anal angle.

Exp. $2\frac{2}{10}$ inches. *Hab.* Rio de Janeiro.

In the Collection of W. C. Hewitson.

This species is remarkable for want of elegance in the contour of its wings, which together are almost as semicircular as in some species of *Euplœa*.

29. Eudamus Pausias.

Alis utrinque rufis : posticis maculis duabus fuscis pone medium.

UPPERSIDE rufous, darker towards the outer margin of the anterior wing. Posterior wing with two small brown spots below the middle.

UNDERSIDE as above.

Exp. 1½ inch. *Hab.* Amazon.

In the Collection of W. C. Hewitson.

30. Eudamus decoratus.

Alis aurantiacis, maculis nigris : anticis margine exteriori late fuscis, lineis longitudinalibus flavis.

UPPERSIDE orange, with bands and spots of black : the abdomen orange banded with black. Anterior wing with two spots near the base, a band before the middle, a triangular spot on the costal margin beyond the middle : the apex and outer margin broadly brown, crossed longitudinally by fine hastate yellow lines. Posterior wing with a spot at the base, two before the middle, and two submarginal bands of spots pyriform near the apex.

UNDERSIDE as above, except that the black spots are larger and that the anal angle of the posterior wing is black.

Exp. 1$\frac{4}{10}$ inch. *Hab.* Sylhet and Java.

In the Collection of W. C. Hewitson.

There is not in the whole family of the *Hesperidæ* a more beautiful species than this.

31. Eudamus Phasias.

Alis ochraceo-fuscis : anticis fasciis duabus macularibus fuscis : posticis macula fasciaque fuscis : infra rufo-fuscis.

UPPERSIDE brown, covered with ochreous hair on the basal half of the anterior wing and the whole of the posterior wing. Anterior wing with two very small transparent

spots at the middle, and a submarginal band of spots chiefly
at the apex, all rufous : the lobe black.

Exp. 1$\frac{1}{10}$ inch. *Hab.* Amazon.

In the Collection of H. W. Bates.

40. Thecla Viceta.

UPPERSIDE. *Male.*—Anterior wing dark brown, the
inner margin at the base cerulean blue, narrow : the discal
spot pale brown, unusually small, within the cell. Posterior
wing with one tail : cerulean blue : the costal margin
rufous-brown, broad : the outer margin darker brown,
narrow.

UNDERSIDE. Anterior wing rufous, tinted with carmine,
crossed beyond the middle by a band of white, bordered inwardly with brown : a submarginal band of very obscure
brown spots. Posterior wing white, with the base rufous-
brown, marked by a spot of white : two or three spots near
the inner margin, a submarginal band of spots indistinct
near the anal angle, a spot on the apex, and the outer margin,
all rufous-brown.

Exp. 1 inch. *Hab.* Amazon.

In the Collection of W. C. Hewitson.

41. Thecla Velina.

UPPERSIDE. *Female.*—Rufous-brown. Posterior wing
with two tails : grey from the base to beyond the middle : a
submarginal line of white at the base of the tails : the
margin dark brown : the lobe rufous.

UNDERSIDE white. Anterior wing crossed beyond the
middle by a rufous band, and near the margin by a band of
rufous spots. Posterior wing with two tails : a large space of
dark red-brown before the middle, angular on its outer border
which is white ; followed by a band of rufous spots, by a
spot of red-brown at the apex, and two smaller spots of the
same colour near the inner margin : the whole of the anal

angle and some submarginal spots rufous : the outer margin
dark brown.

Exp. 1 inch. *Hab.* Amazon (Tapajos).

In the Collection of H. W. Bates.

This and several species following (beautiful things from
the very rich collection of Mr. Bates) form part of the group
to which *T. Crolus* of Cramer belongs.

42. Thecla Verania.

UPPERSIDE. *Male.*—Brilliant dark blue : the margins
(except the apex of the anterior wing, which is broader) dark
brown, narrow.

UNDERSIDE grey-white. Anterior wing crossed beyond
the middle by a rufous band, bordered outwardly with brown
and broken into two parts : a submarginal band of pale
brown spots. Posterior wing crossed at the middle by a band
of seven brick-red spots, bordered on both sides with dark
brown : the first spot near the costal margin, large, the
second (with three below it) also large, the sixth and seventh
forming part of the usual W-like angles : a second band
nearer the outer margin of pale grey spots, two of which near
the apex are much larger than the others : a submarginal band
of rufous spots : the lobe black, bordered above with orange.

Exp. $1\frac{3}{20}$ inch. *Hab.* Amazon.

In the Collection of W. W. Saunders.

43. Thecla Philinna.

UPPERSIDE. *Male.*—Dark brown. Anterior wing with
the basal half (except the costal margin, which is brown)
dull blue : the discal spot large, pale, in two parts, partly in
the cell. Posterior wing with two tails : the apex and outer
margin, which is narrow, dark brown : the lobe scarlet.

UNDERSIDE grey or stone-colour. Both wings crossed
beyond the middle by a band of brick-red spots, bordered
outwardly first with black and then with white, the band of

orange from the base to the middle of the costal margin.
Posterior wing with the base orange, succeeded by a broad
transverse band of silvery white.

Exp. $1\frac{9}{10}$ inch.   *Hab.* Amazon (Ega).

In the collection of W. C. Hewitson, from Mr. Bates.

A very beautiful species, nearly allied to *E. formosus* of
Felder, to be published shortly in the third volume of the
' Novara Voyage.'

36. Eudamus Oriander.

Alis fuscis : anticis maculis vitreis maculisque duabus flavis :
   posticis fasciis duabus macularibus flavis : his infra maculis tribus
   aurantiaco-flavis.

UPPERSIDE dark rufous-brown.   Anterior wing with
seven transparent spots : two at the middle, two outside of
these, and three before the apex : two yellow spots near the
inner margin.   Posterior wing crossed by two bands, each of
three yellow spots.

UNDERSIDE.   Anterior wing as above, except that the
apex is rufous.   Posterior wing rufous, with a round central
spot, and two spots near the inner margin : below the middle
orange-yellow : the anal angle black.

Exp. $1\frac{9}{10}$ inch.   *Hab.* Amazon.

In the Collection of W. C. Hewitson, from Mr. Bates.

Though scarcely different from the last described on the
upperside, it differs greatly below.

37. Eudamus Eous.

Alis fuscis : anticis maculis vitreis maculaque nivea : posticis maculis duabus albis : his infra fascia lata maculaque niveis.

UPPERSIDE dark brown.   Anterior wing with seven
transparent spots : one near the inner margin, two at the
middle, two outside of these, and three before the apex : a
spot of white near the inner margin.   Posterior wing with

two white spots : one before the middle, the other towards the anal angle.

UNDERSIDE. Anterior wing as above, except that there is a white spot on the inner margin touching two of the transparent spots. Posterior wing with a broad central transverse band of white, a linear band on the inner margin and a spot towards the anal angle also white : the anal angle and lobe dark brown.

Exp. 1½ inch. *Hab.* Amazon (Pará).

In the Collection of W. C. Hewitson.

Genus CHÆTOCNEME, *Felder*.

1. Chætocneme Caristus.

Alis ferrugineo-fuscis : anticis fascia lata : posticis margine exteriori late aurantiacis.

UPPERSIDE rufous-brown : the body and wings thickly clothed with rufous hair. Anterior wing crossed at the middle by a broad band of orange. Posterior wing with the outer margin (except the apex, which is dark brown) broadly orange.

UNDERSIDE as above, except that it is of a glossy dark brown.

Exp. 2$\frac{4}{10}$ inches. *Hab.* Aru.

In the Collection of W. C. Hewitson, from Mr. Wallace.

2. Chætocneme Callixenus.

Alis fuscis : anticis fascia lata aurantiaca.

UPPERSIDE dark brown. Anterior wing crossed from the costal to the outer margin by a broad band of orange.

UNDERSIDE as above.

Exp. 2$\frac{3}{10}$ inches. *Hab.* Dorey.

In the Collection of W. C. Hewitson, from Mr. Wallace.

Genus NETROCORYNE, *Felder*.

1. Netrocoryne beata.

Alis rufis: anticis in medio fascia lata quadripartita punctisque
duobus vitreis brunneo marginatis: posticis maculis vitreis tribus:
infra maculis vitreis lilacino marginatis.

UPPERSIDE orange-rufous. Anterior wing sinuated below
the apex: with six transparent spots: four, three of which are
large, in a central band, and two (minute) outside of these,
all bordered with rufous-brown: a brown spot near the base.
Posterior wing with three transparent spots placed in two
bands of brown.

UNDERSIDE as above, except that it is darker, that the
transparent spots of the anterior wing are bordered with lilac,
and that the posterior wing is crossed by a band of lilac and
has the outer margin dark brown.

Exp. $2\frac{2}{10}$ inches. *Hab*. Australia.

In the Collection of W. C. Hewitson.

2. Netrocoryne Denitza.

Alis rufis lilacino lavatis: anticis maculis septem vitreis, tribus centralibus magnis rotundatis: posticis maculis fuscis: alis infra purpureo lavatis.

UPPERSIDE rufous-orange tinted with lilac: the fringe
orange. Anterior wing with the costal margin orange: seven
transparent spots bordered with black: four in the centre,
three of which are very large, and three before the apex: a
brown spot near the base. Posterior wing with a central
orange spot surrounded with spots of dark brown: the nervures lilac.

UNDERSIDE as above, except that the anterior wing is
tinted with purple at the middle, and that the posterior wing
(except the base) is of the same colour.

Exp. $2\frac{2}{10}$ inches. *Hab*. Australia (Moreton Bay).

In the Collection of W. C. Hewitson.

I have adopted the last two genera of the Felders, not because there are any structural differences sufficient to divide them from *Eudamus*, but because the eye, which is in many cases the best guide to the formation of genera, at once detects a distinctive character.

Genus HESPERIA.

1. Hesperia Eudega.

Alis rufo-fuscis: anticis maculis sex vitreis maculaque lineari cinerea: posticis macula vitrea: his infra rufis, maculis obscuris brunneis.

UPPERSIDE. *Male.*—Rufous-brown. Anterior wing with six transparent spots: three a little beyond the middle forming a triangle, and three before the apex: a band of grey (indicative of the male) from near the inner margin to the middle: the costal margin from the base to the middle rufous. Posterior wing with one nearly central transparent spot.

UNDERSIDE rufous. Anterior wing tinted with lilac near the apex. Posterior wing with indistinct spots of darker colour.

Exp. 2 inches. *Hab.* Amazon (Pará).

In the Collection of W. C. Hewitson.

2. Hesperia Hyela.

Alis fuscis, ad basin cæruleo-viridibus: posticis utrinque angulo anali late aurantiaco: infra venis viridibus.

UPPERSIDE. *Male.*—Dark brown: the base of both wings blue-green. Posterior wing with the anal angle broadly orange on both sides.

UNDERSIDE lilac-brown, with the nervures green. Anterior wing with the inner margin rufous-yellow.

Exp. $1\frac{8}{10}$ inch. *Hab.* Java.

In the Collection of W. C. Hewitson, from Mr. Wallace.

This species has a great resemblance to *Ismene Benjaminii*.

3. Hesperia Hyrmina.

Alis fuscis : anticis macula discoidali grisea : posticis utrinque angulo anali aurantiaco,

UPPERSIDE. *Male.*—Dark brown. Anterior wing with
an oblong grey discoidal spot. Posterior wing with the anal
angle orange.

UNDERSIDE as above.

Exp. 2 inches. *Hab.* Tondano and Macassar.

In the Collection of W. C. Hewitson, from Mr. Wallace.

4. Hesperia Aroma.

Alis fuscis, basi corporeque cæruleo-viridibus : anticis infra basi
cæruleo-viridi : posticis fascia lata fusca.

UPPERSIDE dark brown, with the body and base of both
wings blue-green.

UNDERSIDE rufous-brown. Anterior wing with the base
blue-green : the inner margin white. Posterior wing crossed
at the middle by a band of darker brown.

Exp. $1\frac{15}{20}$ inch. *Hab.* Pará.

In the Collection of W. C. Hewitson, from Mr. Bates.

Very much like *Eudamus Creteus* of Cramer (plate 284),
from which it differs little except in the form of the antennæ.

5. Hesperia Bræsia.

Alis fuscis : anticis fascia macularum duarum vitrearum : infra marginibus costalibus ad basin albis.

UPPERSIDE. Anterior wing dark brown, with a central
band of two transparent white spots. Posterior wing rufous-
brown.

UNDERSIDE rufous-brown. Anterior wing with the basal

half dark brown: the costal margin from the base to the middle white. Posterior wing with the base white.

Exp. $1\frac{6}{10}$ inch. *Hab.* Pará.

In the Collection of W. C. Hewitson, from Mr. Bates.

6. Hesperia Cynaxa.

Alis fuscis: anticis fascia vitrea alba: infra anticis apice, posticis omnino griseo-viridibus.

UPPERSIDE dark brown. Anterior wing crossed at the middle by a band of three white transparent spots.

UNDERSIDE as above, except that the apical half of the anterior wing and the whole of the posterior wing are of a grey-green with the nervures black.

Exp. $1\frac{9}{10}$ inch. *Hab.* Mexico.

In the Collection of W. C. Hewitson.

Differs considerably from any other species, but is most nearly allied to *H. Itea* of Swainson and *H. Claudianus* of Latreille.

DESCRIPTIONS

OF

ONE HUNDRED NEW SPECIES

OF

HESPERIDÆ.

BY

W. C. HEWITSON.

PART II.

LONDON:

JOHN VAN VOORST, 1 PATERNOSTER ROW.

March 23rd, 1868.

half dark brown : the costal margin from the base to the middle white. Posterior wing with the base white.

Exp. $1\frac{6}{10}$ inch. *Hab.* Pará.

In the Collection of W. C. Hewitson, from Mr. Bates.

6. Hesperia Cynaxa.

Alis fuscis: anticis fascia vitrea alba: infra anticis apice, posticis omnino griseo-viridibus.

UPPERSIDE dark brown. Anterior wing crossed at the middle by a band of three white transparent spots.

UNDERSIDE as above, except that the apical half of the anterior wing and the whole of the posterior wing are of a grey-green with the nervures black.

Exp. $1\frac{9}{10}$ inch. *Hab.* Mexico.

In the Collection of W. C. Hewitson.

Differs considerably from any other species, but is most nearly allied to *H. Itea* of Swainson and *H. Claudianus* of Latreille.

7. Hesperia Hypaepa.

Celænorrhinus Thrax, *Hübner, Zutrage,* figs. 875, 876.

Exp. 2 to $2\frac{1}{2}$ inches. *Hab.* Sumatra and Singapore.

In the Collection of W. C. Hewitson, from Mr. Wallace.

Thrax having been appropriated for a nearly allied species by Linnæus, I have renamed this.

8. Hesperia immaculata.

Alis utrinque rufo-fuscis immaculatis.

UPPER and UNDERSIDE. Both wings of a uniform rufous-brown.

Exp. $1\frac{7}{10}$ inch. *Hab.* Colombia.

In the Collection of Dr. Boisduval.

[*Published March* 20, 1868.]

9. Hesperia Marpesia.

Alis fuscis: anticis maculis octo vitreis maculaque alba: posticis fascia tripartita alba: his infra dimidio basali cinereo, fascia maculari alba, venis nigris.

UPPERSIDE dark brown. Anterior wing with eight transparent white spots: two within the cell, three below these in a line towards the apex, and three before the apex: a white opaque spot near the middle of the costal margin. Posterior wing with a central trifid transparent white band.

UNDERSIDE. Anterior wing as above, except that it is grey-brown towards the outer margin. Posterior wing with the basal half grey: an undefined band of white beyond the middle: the outer margin broadly brown: the nervures black.

Exp. $1\frac{7}{10}$ inch. *Hab*. Amazon.

In the Collection of W. C. Hewitson.

Near to *H. Phyllus* of Cramer.

10. Hesperia Himella.

Alis fuscis, fimbria albo maculata: anticis maculis septem, posticis maculis tribus vitreis: anticis infra macula apicali albo marginata: posticis in medio albis nigro notatis.

UPPERSIDE dark brown, the fringe broad, alternately black and white. Anterior wing with six transparent white spots: one in the cell, three below it in a line towards the apex, and three before the apex: an opaque white spot and a spot of ochreous hair near the inner margin. Posterior wing with a short central band of three transparent spots.

UNDERSIDE. Anterior wing as above, except that there is a large black spot at the apex, bordered outwardly with white. Posterior wing with a large central irregular space of white, deeply sinuated and marked by some minute black spots: some small spots near the base and two on the inner margin also white: the apex rufous-grey.

Exp. $1\frac{1}{2}$ inch. *Hab*. Rio de Janeiro.

In the Collection of W. C. Hewitson.

This species is one of the group to which *H. Abebalus* of Cramer and one which I have described as *H. Lutetia* belong.

11. Hesperia Artona.

Alis fuscis : anticis maculis vitreis, posticis maculis tribus albis separatim positis : anticis infra apice, posticis omnino lilacino-cinereis, fascia maculari venisque albis.

UPPERSIDE dark brown. Anterior wing with six transparent spots : one in the cell, two below it between the median nervules, and three before the apex : a spot of opaque white near the inner margin. Posterior wing with a band of three separate white spots.

UNDERSIDE. Anterior wing as above, except that the apex is lilac-grey. Posterior wing lilac-grey, with the nervures white : crossed below the middle by a band of five white spots.

Exp. 1½ inch. *Hab*. Rio de Janeiro.

In the Collection of W. C. Hewitson.

Near to *H. Plyllus* and *H. Abebalus* of Cramer.

12. Hesperia Dolopia.

Alis fuscis : anticis maculis vitreis, posticis fascia rufescente : infra rufis ; anticis fascia submarginali, posticis margine costali ad basin, linea basali, fascia lata centrali fasciaque submarginali flavo-albis.

UPPERSIDE dark brown. Anterior wing with six transparent white spots : one in the cell, two between the median nervures, and three before the apex : an indistinct rufous submarginal band. Posterior wing with an oblique rufous band before the middle.

UNDERSIDE rufous-brown. Anterior wing with the inner margin and a submarginal band pale yellow. Posterior wing with the costal margin at the base, a narrow band from the base, a broad central band, a spot near the anal angle, and a submarginal band pale yellow : a submarginal band of brown spots.

Exp. $\frac{15}{20}$ inch.   *Hab.* Northern India.
In the Collection of W. C. Hewitson.

Near to *H. Propertius,* Donovan, ' Insects of India,' plate 47.

13. Hesperia Laurea.

Alis fuscis: anticis maculis quinque vitreis maculaque alba; posticis
fascia tripartita alba: infra anticis fascia subapicali flava; posticis
margine costali fasciaque parallela flavis.

UPPERSIDE dark brown.   Anterior wing with five transparent white spots: two at the middle, one outside of these,
and two at the apex: a white opaque spot near the middle of
the inner margin: the inner margin, from the base to the
said spot, lilac-white.   Posterior wing with a trifid white
central spot and a band of white hair near the inner margin.

UNDERSIDE rufous-brown.   Anterior wing crossed near
the apex by a band of yellow.   Posterior wing with the
costal margin (which is broad) and a band parallel to it
yellow.

Exp. $1\frac{1}{2}$ inch.   *Hab.* Rio de Janeiro and Cayenne.
In the Collection of W. C. Hewitson.

Near to *H. Phyllus* of Cramer, plate 176.

14. Hesperia Physcoa.

Alis fuscis: anticis macula minuta vitrea, linea nigra maris: posticis
infra, purpureo tinctis rufo-fùscis macula fasciaque macularum
minutarum rufarum.

UPPERSIDE dark rufous-brown.   Anterior wing with one
minute transparent spot between the second and third median
nervures, a black line (which is scarcely seen) marking the
male.

UNDERSIDE rufous-brown.   Posterior wing tinted with
purple: a central spot and curved band below it of minute
rufous spots.

Exp. $1\frac{2}{10}$ inch.
In the Collection of W. C. Hewitson.

15. Hesperia Homolea.

Alis fuscis: anticis maculis vitreis : anticis infra fascia submarginali, posticis fasciis duabus ochraceis.

UPPERSIDE dark brown. Anterior wing with five transparent spots: one in the cell, two between the median nervures, and two before the apex.

UNDERSIDE. Anterior wing with a submarginal band of ochreous spots. Posterior wing with two bands of similar spots and one spot more distinct than the rest towards the anal angle.

Exp. $1\frac{3}{10}$ inch. *Hab.* Singapore.

In the Collection of W. C. Hewitson, from Mr. Wallace.

16. Hesperia Bononia.

Alis fuscis : anticis maculis quinque, posticis maculis duabus vitreis: infra ochraceis, anticis in medium fuscis.

UPPERSIDE dark brown. Anterior wing with five transparent spots : three between the median nervures and two before the apex : an opaque pale-yellow spot near the costal margin. Posterior wing with two transparent spots.

UNDERSIDE ochreous-yellow : the middle of the anterior wing dark brown. Posterior wing with the transparent spots boadered below with brown, and with a brown spot on each side of them.

Exp. $1\frac{1}{10}$ inch. *Hab.* Singapore.

In the Collection of W. C. Hewitson, from Mr. Wallace.

17. Hesperia Anthea.

Alis fuscis: anticis maculis vitreis, posticis fascia lata alba ex margine interiori ad medium alæ ; his infra fascia latiori et longiori.

UPPERSIDE dark brown. Anterior wing with five small transparent white spots : two between the median nervures and three before the apex. Posterior wing with a broad band of white from the inner margin to the middle : the fringe white.

UNDERSIDE as above, except that the white band is broader and crosses the whole of the wing.

Exp. 1$\frac{3}{10}$ inch.   *Hab.* Singapore.

In the Collection of W. C. Hewitson, from Mr. Wallace.

Near to *H. azona* and *H. Elia.*

18. Hesperia fusina.

Alis rufo-fuscis : anticis maculis vitreis : posticis infra fascia angusta maculari lilacino-alba.

UPPERSIDE dark rufous-brown.   Anterior wing with six transparent spots : three at the middle, one of which is triangular, two (very minute) before the apex, and one (yellow) near the costal margin.

UNDERSIDE paler.   Anterior wing as above.   Posterior wing crossed beyond the middle by a narrow band of lilac-white spots.

Exp. 1$\frac{7}{10}$ inch.   *Hab.* Amazon (Santarem).

In the Collection of W. C. Hewitson.

Near to *H. xanthaphes* of Hübner's 'Sammlung.' A specimen in my Collection (it may be a variety of this or distinct) differs from it only in having the band on the underside of the posterior wing much broader.

19. Hesperia avesta.

Alis fuscis: anticis maculis duabus vitreis : his infra macula costali flava ; posticis fascia ante medium flava.

UPPERSIDE dark brown.   Anterior wing with two central transparent spots.

UNDERSIDE rufous-brown.   Anterior wing with the outer margin broadly grey : a yellow spot at the middle of the costal margin.   Posterior wing with a transverse band of yellow before the middle.

Exp. 1$\frac{6}{10}$ inch.   *Hab.* Sumatra.

In the Collection of W. C. Hewitson.

Unlike any other species I know.

20. Hesperia feralia.

Alis fuscis: anticis maculis septem vitreis, posticis macula tripartita vitrea.

UPPERSIDE dark brown. Anterior wing with seven transparent spots: two within the cell, one below these quadrate produced in a line towards the middle of the inner margin, and two outside of these near the two subapical spots. Posterior wing with a central trifid transparent spot.

UNDERSIDE as above, except that it is rufous-brown.

Exp. $1\frac{13}{20}$ inch. *Hab.* Java.

In the Collection of Dr. Boisduval.

21. Hesperia palæa.

Alis fuscis: anticis linea (maris) centrali fracta alba: his infra macula flava costali.

UPPERSIDE dark brown. Anterior wing with a broken line of white (marking the male).

UNDERSIDE rufous-brown. Anterior wing with a spot of pale yellow near the middle of the inner margin.

Exp. $1\frac{8}{10}$ inch.

In the Collection of Dr. Boisduval.

22. Hesperia Oceia.

Alis fuscis: anticis maculis vitreis: posticis plaga ovali media rugoso-squamosa setis longis nigris decumbentibus obtecta.

UPPERSIDE dark rufous-brown. Anterior wing with seven transparent spots: two, very small, within the cell, three between the nervures below these, and two before the apex. Posterior wing with a large tuft of black hair below the costal margin.

Exp. $1\frac{6}{10}$ inch. *Hab.* Philippines.

In the Collection of W. C. Hewitson.

23. Hesperia Phigalia.

Alis fuscis: anticis maculis sex aurantiacis maculaque flava, posticis
fascia lata aurantiaca : anticis infra apice, posticis omnino cinereis,
his maculis annulatis nigris.

UPPERSIDE dark brown. Anterior wing with six orange-
yellow transparent spots, three of which are large and central,
and one opaque spot of pale yellow. Posterior wing with a
short broad band of orange-yellow : the fringe broad, grey.

UNDERSIDE grey: anterior wing with the centre dark
brown, the base orange-yellow. Posterior wing with a
central spot, and below it a semicircle of annular misshapen
black spots.

Exp. $1\frac{7}{20}$ inch. *Hab.* Australia.

In the Collection of W. C. Hewitson.

Near *Symmomus* of Hübner's 'Zutrage,' f. 225.

24. Hesperia Eliena.

Alis rufo-fuscis: anticis maculis vitreis, posticis fascia tripartita
flava : posticis infra maculis quinque albis nigro marginatis.

UPPERSIDE rufous-brown. Anterior wing with six transparent spots and one pale-yellow opaque spot. Posterior
wing with a central trifid band of yellow.

UNDERSIDE with the apex of the anterior wing and the
whole of the posterior wing rufous. Posterior wing with five
round silvery-white spots bordered with black : one in the
middle, and four (one of which is apart from the others)
forming a band below the middle.

Exp. $1\frac{1}{2}$ inch. *Hab.* Australia (Moreton Bay).

In the Collection of W. C. Hewitson.

25. Hesperia Petalia.

Alis rufo-fuscis: anticis maculis vitreis maculaque flava, posticis
macula flava: anticis infra apice, posticis omnino rufo-cinereis, his
macula nigra albo notata.

UPPERSIDE glossy rufous-brown, with six pale-yellow

transparent spots and one spot of opaque yellow. Posterior wing with a central yellow spot.

UNDERSIDE with the apex of the anterior wing and the whole of the posterior wing pale rufous-grey. Posterior wing with a large central round black spot : its centre white.

Exp. $1\frac{5}{20}$ inch. *Hab.* Australia (Moreton Bay).

In the Collection of W. C. Hewitson.

Also near to *Symmomus*.

26. Hesperia Liburnia.

Alis fuscis : anticis maculis septem (una in medio magna) vitreo-fulvis maculaque subbasali aurantiaca, posticis fascia lata cili-isque aurantiacis : anticis infra fascia submarginali macularum flavidarum, posticis margine costali maculisque decem au-rantiacis.

UPPERSIDE dark brown. Anterior wing with seven transparent glossy orange-yellow spots : one large and bifid before the middle, three between this and the apex, one above these near the costal margin, and two before the apex : two or three lines from the base and a spot near the inner margin (opaque) also orange-yellow ; the fringe brown, except near the anal angle, where it is yellow. Posterior wing with a central short broad band, some hair at the base, a band parallel and near to the inner margin, and the fringe orange-yellow.

UNDERSIDE dark brown. Anterior wing with the spots as above : the three spots nearest the base joined in one, the three spots between these and the apex also joined : a line on the costal margin and a band of hastate submarginal spots also orange-yellow. Posterior wing with two bands from the base, a spot between them, the costal margin from the base to the middle, a subcostal band, the central band as above, and a submarginal band of five spots, all brilliant orange-yellow. Abdomen banded with yellow.

Exp. $1\frac{1}{2}$ inch. *Hab.* Philippines.

In the Collection of W. C. Hewitson.

A very beautiful species, near to *H. flavescens* of Felder, nearer to the following, from which it does not differ, except on the underside.

27. Hesperia Latoia.

Alis fuscis: anticis maculis septem vitreo-flavis maculaque aurantiaca, posticis fascia lata vitrea ciliisque aurantiacis: anticis
infra fascia submarginali *venis*que fulvis, posticis venis fasciaque
submarginali macularum minutarum fulvis.

UPPERSIDE dark brown. Anterior wing with seven transparent pale-yellow spots: one large and bifid, three between
this and the apex (the last very minute), one near the middle
of the costal margin, and two before the apex: two lines from
the base and a spot near the inner margin orange-yellow:
the fringe (except at the anal angle, where it is yellow)
brown. Posterior wing with a broad central band, some
hair at the base, and a line parallel and near to the inner
margin orange-yellow.

UNDERSIDE as above, except that the nervures are
orange-yellow, that the anterior wing has an orange linear
band at the costal margin, and that the posterior wing has
the central band longer and a submarginal band of minute
orange spots. Abdomen banded with yellow.

Exp. $1\frac{4}{10}$ inch. *Hab.* Singapore.

In the Collection of W. C. Hewitson, from Mr. Wallace.

Differs from *H. Liburnia* chiefly in having the nervures
of the underside yellow.

28. Hesperia Heræa.

Alis nigro-fuscis: anticis basi, macula cellulari, fascia obliqua
macularum quatuor maculaque apicali bifida aurantiacis; posticis
utrinque aurantiacis margine costali et interiori, angulo anali
fasciaque basali fuscis: his infra maculis fuscis, marginibus rufis.

UPPERSIDE dark brown, with the fringe orange. Anterior wing with the base, the costal and inner margins to the

middle, a broad oblique band from the inner margin towards the apex, a spot within the cell, and two spots before the apex orange. Posterior wing orange, with the costal and inner margins, a linear spot between them, and the anal angle dark brown.

UNDERSIDE. Anterior wing as above, except tnat it is rufous towards the apex and outer margin. Posterior wing orange-yellow, with the margins and a spot near the middle rufous : a band near the inner margin, a bifid spot near the middle, and three spots towards the anal angle dark brown.

Exp. $1\frac{3}{10}$ inch. *Hab.* Amazon (Ega).

In the Collection of W. C. Hewitson, from Mr. Bates.

Near to *H. flavescens* of Felder, from which it scarcely differs above.

29. Hesperia Laronia.

Alis aurantiacis : anticis basi margineque costali rufescente, macula subapicali margineque exteriori fuscis ; posticis macula discali margineque exteriori fuscis : his infra maculis tribus albis nigro marginatis.

UPPERSIDE orange. Anterior wing with the base and costal margin rufous : a large spot (sinuated on both sides) near the apex, and the outer margin (which is broad), dark brown. Posterior wing with a brown spot before the middle and the outer margin (which is narrow) dark brown : the inner margin rufous.

UNDERSIDE as above, except that it is paler, that the outer margin of the anterior wing is ochreous-brown, and that the base of the posterior wing is clouded with ochreous-brown, and marked with three white spots bordered with black.

Exp. $1\frac{2}{10}$ inch. *Hab.* Old Calabar.

In the Collection of W. C. Hewitson.

Unlike any other known species.

30. Hesperia Galatia.

Alis ochraceis, fusco irroratis: anticis macula discali, apice margineque exteriori fuscis, linea obliqua recta nigra: infra omnino rufis.

UPPERSIDE ochreous, irrorated with brown. Anterior wing crossed beyond the middle from above the anal angle to a little beyond the end of the cell by a straight black line: a spot at the end of the cell, the outer margin and the nervures near it dark brown. Posterior wing with the costal margin broadly dark brown: the outer margin narrow, dark brown.

UNDERSIDE rufous, except the base of the anterior wing, which is dark brown.

Exp. $1\frac{5}{20}$ inch. *Hab.* Old Calabar.

In the Collection of W. C. Hewitson.

Unlike any other known species.

31. Hesperia Beturia.

Alis fuscis: anticis maculis quatuor vitreis: his infra margine costali flavo irrorato, fascia subapicali macularum flavidarum; posticis fasciis duabus macularum flavidarum.

UPPERSIDE dark brown with four transparent white spots: two near the middle, and two before the apex: the base and the middle of the posterior wing covered with ochreous hair.

UNDERSIDE paler brown. Both wings with a submarginal band of pale-yellow spots. Anterior wing with the costal margin broadly irrorated with yellow. Posterior wing irrorated with yellow near the base: crossed at the middle by a band of yellow spots.

Exp. $1\frac{4}{10}$ inch. *Hab.* Neilgherries and Macassar from Mr. Wallace.

In the Collection of W. C. Hewitson.

32. Hesperia Utha.

Alis nigro-fuscis dimidio basali fulvo: anticis fascia maculari sub-apicali fulva, posticis ciliis fulvis: his infra rufo-fuscis macula fasciaque rufis.

UPPERSIDE dark brown, with the base of both wings rufous-orange: the nervures black. Anterior wing with a band of spots of the same colour before the apex. Posterior wing with the fringe rufous.

UNDERSIDE. Anterior wing as above, except that the base is dark brown. Posterior wing rufous-brown, with a rufous spot before the middle and a band of spots of the same colour at the middle.

Exp. $1\frac{9}{10}$ inch. *Hab.* Cuba.

In the Collection of W. C. Hewitson.

Near to *H. Zabulon* of the United States, but twice the size.

33. Hesperia ficulnea.

Alis fuscis: anticis macula magna discali lilacino-alba.

UPPERSIDE dark brown. Anterior wing with one large central white spot tinted with lilac.

UNDERSIDE as above, except that it is paler.

Exp. $1\frac{6}{10}$ inch. *Hab.* Borneo.

In the Collection of W. C. Hewitson.

Genus HESPERILLA, *Hewitson.*

Body robust, as long or longer than the wings. Head large. Palpi with the last joint bare, and projecting beyond the dense hair with which the other joints are covered. Antennæ of moderate length, slightly curved, spotted with white, the club long and curved, as in *Eudamus*: also like *Pyrrhopyga*, but more pointed and slender. Anterior wing with the apex pointed: crossed, as in *Hesperia*, by the band indicative of the male: the first branch of the median

nervure not distant from the second. Posterior wing with
the third branch of the median nervure leaving it at an
angle from which the cell is closed in a straight line.
The hind legs with four spurs. Type *P. ornata*, Leach.
The insects of this genus have all the characteristics of
Hesperia except the antennæ.

1. Hesperilla Halyzia.

Alis fuscis, ciliis albis: anticis maculis tribus discalibus vitreis:
anticis infra margine costali apiceque, posticis omnino cinerareis,
his maculis fuscis parum visis.

UPPERSIDE dark brown: the fringe white, spotted with
brown on the anterior wing. Anterior wing with three
central transparent spots: the base of the costal margin
grey.

UNDERSIDE cinereous, except the lower half of the
anterior wing, which is dark brown. Posterior wing crossed
by some very indistinct brown spots beyond the middle.

Exp. $1\frac{3}{10}$ inch. *Hab.* Australia (Port Denison).

In the Collection of W. C. Hewitson.

This species is without the mark peculiar to the male.

2. Hesperilla Dirphia.

Alis fuscis: anticis maculis septem separatim dispositis: posticis
infra macula alba maculisque tribus nonnunquam fuscis nonnunquam albo maculatis.

UPPERSIDE. Female dark brown. Anterior wing with
seven opaque white spots: two near the middle widely apart,
two together outside of these, and three before the apex.
Posterior wing with the basal half thickly clothed with hair.

UNDERSIDE rufous. Anterior wing as above, except
that it is without the apical spots. Posterior wing with a
central spot of white above the middle, bordered with brown,
and below the middle a band of three spots, sometimes

brown only, sometimes having each spot marked with
white.

Exp. 1$\frac{11}{20}$ inch. *Hab.* Australia (Swan River).

In the Collection of W. C. Hewitson.

3. Hesperilla Donnysa.

Alis fuscis, maculis sex vitreo-flavis maculaque minuta flava, posticis
in medio aurantiacis : his infra griseis macula fasciaque macularum
fuscis.

UPPERSIDE. *Male.*—Anterior wing rufous-brown, with
six transparent yellow spots: one near the middle of the
costal margin, two central beyond the middle, and three
before the apex : a small yellow spot near the inner margin,
and the black line indicative of the male. Posterior wing
dark brown, with the centre orange.

UNDERSIDE grey. Anterior wing with the basal half
dark brown : a ray of yellow from the base to the first transparent spot: the inner margin yellow in the place of the
small yellow spot of the upperside. Posterior wing with a
spot before the middle, followed by a straight band of small
brown spots.

Female without the small yellow spot of the anterior
wing and the central orange of the posterior wing.

Exp. 1$\frac{5}{20}$ inch. *Hab.* Australia (Moreton Bay).

In the Collection of W. C. Hewitson.

4. Hesperilla Doclea.

Alis rufo-fuscis : anticis macula oblonga in cellula maculisque
tribus minutis vitreis, vitta maris lata nigra : posticis infra griseo
irroratis.

UPPERSIDE. *Male.*—Rufous-brown. Anterior wing with
five transparent spots : one oblong in the cell, one between
the median nervules, and three (very minute) before the

apex : crossed obliquely from the inner margin by a broad black band indicative of the male.

UNDERSIDE as above, except that it is paler and irrorated throughout with grey.

Exp. 1$\frac{5}{20}$ inch. *Hab.* Australia (Moreton Bay).

In the Collection of W. C. Hewitson.

Closely resembling in character the *Hesperiæ* of Europe, and *H. comma* and *Cernes* of the United States.

Genus CYCLOPIDES, *Hübner*.

CARTEROCEPHALUS, *Lederer*.

1. Cyclopides Caicus.

Alis fuscis : anticis maculis sex vitreis maculaque opaca albis, posticis macula magna discali alba : his infra macula discali maculis duabus tripartitis subcostalibus ochraceis : maculis duabus prope angulum analem albis.

UPPERSIDE dark brown. Anterior wing with six transparent white spots : two near the middle (one below the other), one beyond these, and three at the apex. Posterior wing with one large central silvery-white spot.

UNDERSIDE. Anterior wing as above, except that the costal and outer margins are rufous, the apex marked by two pale rufous spots, and that the two lowest white spots are united in one. Posterior wing rufous, with the central spot as above, two large ochreous trifid spots at the costal margin, two white spots near the anal angle, and a submarginal band of four small rufous spots.

Exp. 1$\frac{5}{20}$ inch. *Hab.* Venezuela.

In the Collection of W. C. Hewitson.

Very near to *C. cypselus* of Felder.

2. Cyclopides Cænides.

Alis fuscis, ciliis rufis: anticis maculis sex vitreo-fulvis, posticis macula magna aurantiaco-fulva: his infra rufis immaculatis.

UPPERSIDE rufous-brown, darker towards the outer margin of the posterior wing: the fringe rufous. Anterior wing with six transparent orange spots : three longitudinally at the middle of the wing and three (very minute) near the apex. Posterior wing with a large oblong orange spot before the middle.

UNDERSIDE. Anterior wing as above, but paler near the margins. Posterior wing rufous, irrorated with paler colour.

Exp. 1 inch. *Hab.* Venezuela.

In the Collection of W. C. Hewitson.

Nearly allied to *C. cypselus* of Felder.

3. Cyclopides Carmides.

Alis fuscis: anticis maculis tribus vitreis in triangulum dispositis, posticis macula fasciaque aurantiacis: his infra macula argentea.

UPPERSIDE. Dark brown, with rufous hair at the base. Anterior wing tinted with purple towards the outer margin, with three central transparent spots placed in the form of a triangle. Posterior wing with an orange spot before the middle, and beyond it a band of three spots of the same colour.

UNDERSIDE rufous-brown. Anterior wing as above, except that part of the inner margin is pale. Posterior wing with a large silvery central spot.

Exp. 1$\frac{8}{10}$ inch. *Hab.* Madagascar.

In the Collection of W. C. Hewitson.

4. Cyclopides argenteo-ornatus.

Alis fuscis: anticis maculis septem aurantiaco-flavis, posticis macula oblonga aurantiaca: his infra viridibus, maculis quatuor fasciaque argenteo-albis.

UPPERSIDE. Dark brown, the base clothed with rufous

hair: the fringe broad, black and white. Anterior wing with seven opaque orange-yellow spots: four central large, near together, and three before the apex. Posterior wing with an oblong orange spot.

UNDERSIDE ochreous-green. Anterior wing with the spots as above. Posterior wing *with four oblong spots and a band of silver-white,* and the orange spot as above.

Exp. 1$\frac{5}{20}$ inch. *Hab.* Australia (Swan River).

In the Collection of W. C. Hewitson.

5. Cyclopides Cheles.

Alis fuscis: anticis fasciis duabus submarginalibus macularum fla- vidarum: posticis subtus flavidis, tessellatis.

UPPERSIDE dark brown. Anterior wing with two sub- marginal bands of pale-yellow spots, the inner band shortest, broken, its spots seven in number, placed three together (at the costal margin): the rest in pairs.

UNDERSIDE. Anterior wing as above, except that the outer submarginal band is shorter, and the inner band absent, except the three spots near the costal margin, which are minute. Posterior wing pale yellow, with the nervures, some short lines near the costal margin, two transverse lines at the middle (forming spots), and a submarginal line all dark brown.

Exp. 1$\frac{5}{20}$ inch. *Hab.* Damara Land.

In the Collection of W. C. Hewitson.

Its nearest neighbour is *C. Steropes.*

6. Cyclopides Callicles.

Alis fuscis maculis quinquedecim flavidis: anticis novem, posticis maculis sex: his infra flavis, macula centrali maculisque septem pallidioribus in semicirculum positis nigro marginatis.

UPPERSIDE dark brown, with pale yellow semitrans- parent spots. Anterior wing with nine, posterior wing with six—one in the middle, five in a band below.

UNDERSIDE yellow. Anterior wing with the lower half
dark brown; the spots on the yellow portion of the wing
bordered with black. Posterior wing with two black spots
near the base, the central spot and seven spots below it
bordered with black.

Exp. 1$\frac{2}{10}$ inch. *Hab.* Damara Land.

In the Collection of W. C. Hewitson.

Like *Hesperia* above, but resembling *C. Steropes* underneath.

7. Cyclopides Capenas.

Alis fuscis: anticis maculis magnis quatuor venisque pone medium
flavidis: posticis subtus flavidis maculis atris sparsis.

UPPERSIDE dark brown. Anterior wing with four large
spots and the nervures towards the outer margin yellow.
Posterior wing with four yellow spots (one bifid).

UNDERSIDE. Anterior wing as above, except that the
costal margin and a line before the fringe are yellow.
Posterior wing yellow, with numerous irregular black spots.

Exp. 1$\frac{1}{20}$ inch. *Hab.* Zambesi.

In the Collection of W. C. Hewitson.

Nearest to *P. Macoma* of Trimen.

8. Cyclopides Camertes.

Alis fuscis: anticis maculis quatuor (tribus maximis) fulvis, posticis
macula magna trifida: his infra fulvis maculis fuscis sparcis.

UPPERSIDE dark brown. Anterior wing with four
orange-yellow spots, three of which are very large (one
bifid). Posterior wing with one large trifid orange-yellow
spot.

UNDERSIDE. Anterior wing as above, except that the
apex is yellow, spotted with brown. Posterior wing orange-
yellow, with many irregular brown spots.

Exp. 1 inch. *Hab.* Singapore.

In the Collection of W. C. Hewitson, from Mr. Wallace.

9. Cyclopides Cariate.

Alis rufo-fuscis: anticis maculis septem aurantiacis in forma *Y* positis: posticis ochraceis maculis quatuor pallidioribus parum visis.

UPPERSIDE rufous-brown. Anterior wing with seven opaque orange spots, placed in the form of the letter *Y*: three forming a central band, three from the middle of the costal margin which join the band, and one at the apex.

UNDERSIDE. Anterior wing as above, except that the margins are broadly rufous. Posterior wing rufous, with four indistinct paler spots in pairs.

Exp. ♂ $\frac{9}{10}$, ♀ $1\frac{2}{10}$ inch. *Hab.* Madagascar.

In the Collection of W. C. Hewitson.

Near to *C. Rhadama* of Boisduval.

10. Cyclopides Ceramas.

Alis rufo-fuscis, ciliis latis pallidis: anticis maculis octo fulvis, posticis maculis quatuor: anticis infra apice, posticis omnino ochraceis, maculis flavis notatis.

UPPERSIDE rufous-brown. Anterior wing with eight minute orange spots: one in the cell, three at the apex, two below these, and two nearer the outer margin. Posterior wing with four spots in pairs.

UNDERSIDE. Anterior wing as above, except that the costal margin and apex and the whole of the posterior wing are ochreous-yellow. Posterior wing with some indistinct spots of a brighter yellow.

Exp. $\frac{15}{20}$ inch. *Hab.* Neilgherries.

In the Collection of W. C. Hewitson.

Also very near to *Rhadama,* but with the yellow spots differently placed.

Genus ANCYLOXIPHA, *Felder*.

1. Ancyloxipha aurantiaca.

Alis utrinque aurantiaco-fulvis, basibus fuscis.

UPPERSIDE orange-yellow, with the base of both wings brown.

UNDERSIDE as above.

Exp. $\frac{7}{10}$ inch.

In the Collection of W. C. Hewitson.

2. Ancyloxipha Ardonia.

Alis rufo-fuscis: anticis maculis novem flavidis, posticis macula cellulari fasciaque quadripartita flavis.

UPPERSIDE rufous-brown, the fringe yellow. Anterior wing with nine pale-yellow spots: one in the cell nearly bifid, five forming an oblique band in the middle, two of which are apart from the other three, three before the apex and a line on the inner margin. Posterior wing with a small spot in the cell and a band of four spots in the middle pale yellow.

UNDERSIDE with the spots as above. Both wings with a submarginal band of large pale-yellow spots: the costal margin and apex of the anterior wing and the whole of the posterior wing irrorated with ochreous-yellow.

Exp. $\frac{9}{10}$ inch. *Hab.* Macassar and Sarawak.

In the Collection of W. C. Hewitson, from Mr. Wallace.

3. Ancyloxipha agraulia.

Alis fuscis: anticis macula magna costali, margine interiori, fascia transversa, maculaque subapicali vix tripartita aurantiacis: posticis pilis basalibus, macula parva costali fasciaque transversa aurantiacis.

UPPERSIDE dark brown. Anterior wing with a large space on the costal margin, the inner margin, a transverse band from it to near the apex, and the three subapical spots scarcely divided from each other orange. Posterior wing with some hair at the base, a small spot near the costal margin, and a transverse band orange.

UNDERSIDE as above, except that the apex of the anterior wing and the whole of the posterior wing are rufous, and the bands less distinct.

Exp. $\frac{17}{20}$ inch. *Hab.* Australia (Swan River).

In the Collection of W. C. Hewitson.

Genus LEUCOCHITONEA, *Wallengren.*

1. Leucochitonea Lucullea.

Alis fuscis : anticis cæruleo irroratis, fascia subbasali nigra ; posticis fasciis duabus viridi-cæruleis : his infra cæruleis, maculis discalibus, macula apicali albo notata, maculisque submarginalibus nigro-fuscis.

UPPERSIDE dark brown. Anterior wing irrorated throughout with pale blue : ten transparent spots : four (one deeply sinuated) in the middle of the wing, one (bifid) below these, and five before the apex placed irregularly and apart : a transverse black band near the base : the fringe brown. Posterior wing crossed by two transverse bands of blue-green ; the fringe white.

UNDERSIDE. Anterior wing dark brown, with the base blue, a large spot on the inner margin and a band of submarginal spots white. Posterior wing cerulean blue, with three spots in the middle, a spot at the apex marked by two white spots, and a submarginal band of spots all dark brown : the outer margin brown, dentated on its inner border.

Exp. $1\frac{3}{20}$ inch. *Hab.* Amazon (Ega).

In the Collection of W. C. Hewitson.

Near to *L. Cerealis.*

2. Leucochitonea Libethra.

Alis anticis rufo-fuscis, maculis decem vitreis; posticis griseo-
rufis, basi nigro-fusca, maculis quatuor albis subbasalibus: his
infra cæruleis, macula magna costali nigro-fusca, maculis margineque exteriori fuscis.

UPPERSIDE rufous-brown. Anterior wing irrorated with
pale blue: ten transparent white spots: three near the middle
of the costal margin, three below these in the middle of the
wing, and four near the apex, forming a square: the fringe
brown. Posterior wing rufous-grey, with the base dark
brown, and a spot at the anal angle (touching which there
are four white spots) also brown: the fringe white.

UNDERSIDE. Anterior wing as above. Posterior wing
pale blue irrorated with black, with a large black spot on the
costal margin, two or three smaller spots, and the outer
margin, which is broad, brown.

Exp. $1\frac{2}{10}$ inch. *Hab.* Amazon (St. Paulo).

In the Collection of W. C. Hewitson.

Also near *L. Cerealis.*

3. Leucochitonea Lagia.

Pythonides Herennius, *Hübner, Sammlung*, figs. 1, 2, 3, 4.

I have renamed this, the specific name having been previously used by Cramer.

4. Leucochitonea lancea.

Carystus Jovianus, *Hübner, Zutrage*, figs. 713, 714.

Not believing this to be the same species as *Jovianus* of
Cramer, I have given it another name.

5. Leucochitonea Limæa.

Alis fuscis: anticis cæruleo irroratis, posticis margine exteriori late
cæruleo: his infra cæruleis, apice rufo-fusco.

UPPERSIDE. Anterior wing irrorated with blue, the blue forming a spot in the cell, a spot on the costal margin beyond the middle, and a submarginal band, all very inditinct. Posterior wing with the outer margin broadly blue.

UNDERSIDE. Anterior wing as above, but paler. Posterior wing blue, with the apex rufous-brown.

Exp. $1\frac{3}{10}$ inch. *Hab.* Cayenne.

In the Collection of W. C. Hewitson.

6. Leucochitonea Lerina.

Alis fuscis: anticis maculis quatuor discalibus albo-vitreis, fascia submarginali macularum cærulearum, posticis fascia lata cærulea: his infra cæruleis, venis, maculis duabus margineque exteriori fuscis.

UPPERSIDE dark brown, the fringe brown. Anterior wing with four transparent white spots at the middle of the wing, and a band of blue spots towards the outer margin. Posterior wing crossed before the middle by a broad band of cerulean blue.

UNDERSIDE. Anterior wing as above. Posterior wing cerulean blue, with the nervures, two spots before the middle, and the outer margin dark brown.

Exp. $1\frac{5}{20}$ inch. *Hab.* Cayenne and Pará.

In the Collection of W. C. Hewitson.

7. Leucochitonea Laginia.

L. niveus ♂, *Hübner, Sammlung,* figs. 1, 2.

8. Leucochitonea Laviana.

Alis niveis: anticis apice late fusco, maculis albis notato, margine exteriori maculis fuscis albo marginatis: posticis infra maculis duabus, linea margineque exteriori rufo-fuscis.

UPPERSIDE white, with the base brown. Anterior wing with the apex broadly brown, crossed by a broad band of white and by two subapical bands of minute white spots:

the outer margin below these marked by lunular brown spots bordered with white. Posterior wing with the outer margin and some lunular spots upon it dark brown.

UNDERSIDE. Anterior wing as above, except that the apex is marked by a distinct triangular spot. Posterior wing with a large spot near the costal margin, a spot near the middle, a linear band beyond the middle, and the outer margin brown.

Exp. 1$\frac{6}{10}$ inch. *Hab.* Nicaragua.

In the Collection of W. C. Hewitson.

Near to *L. Arsalte.*

9. Leucochitonea Leucola.

Alis albis: anticis apice, margine exteriori venisque pone medium fuscis: posticis infra fascia, apice, venis lineisque inter eas fuscis.

UPPERSIDE white. Anterior wing with the base, the apex and outer margin, which are broad, and the nervures near it dark brown : a subapical band of white divided by the nervures. Posterior wing with the outer margin and the nervures beyond the middle dark brown : the fringe brown, traversed by a line of white.

UNDERSIDE. Anterior wing as above. Posterior wing with the base, a band before the middle, the apex, the nervures, and lines between them brown.

Exp. 1$\frac{3}{10}$ inch. *Hab.* Minas Geraes.

In the Collection of W. C. Hewitson.

Also near to *L. Arsalte.*

10. Leucochitonea Lassia.

Alis obscure albis, fasciis duabus submarginalibus rufo-fuscis : anticis basi rufo-fusca, apice maculis quatuor vitreis albis.

UPPERSIDE obscure white. Both wings with two submarginal bands of rufous-brown. Anterior wing irrorated with brown, the base and a band of darker colour which crosses it brown: four subapical transparent white spots: the space between the submarginal bands tinted with lilac.

UNDERSIDE as above, except that the submarginal bands are broken into spots and less distinct.

Exp. $1\frac{9}{20}$ inch.

In the Collection of W. C. Hewitson.

Belongs to the same group as *P. Melander* of Cramer.

11. Leucochitonea trifasciata.

Alis pallide rufis, anticis lilacino tinctis, ambabus fasciis tribus margineque exteriori rufo-fuscis.

UPPERSIDE rufous, pale, tinted with lilac on the anterior wing. Both wings crossed by three bands of brown, both with the outer margin brown. Anterior wing with the first band broad, the second angular, the third and submarginal band macular.

UNDERSIDE as above, except that it is much paler, and that the anterior wing is without the subbasal band.

Exp. $1\frac{1}{2}$ inch.

In the Collection of W. C. Hewitson.

Belongs to the same group as the last, but very distinct.

12. Leucochitonea Lucaria.

Alis fuscis: anticis cinereo tinctis, macula costali maculaque anali fulvis, posticis fascia submarginali fulva.

UPPERSIDE dark brown. Anterior wing tinted with lilac-grey towards the outer margin: an oblong spot from the middle of the costal margin, and a small spot near the anal angle, yellow. Posterior wing with a band of yellow near the outer margin.

UNDERSIDE as above, except that the spot near the anal

angle is larger and that there is a similar spot at the anal angle of the posterior wing.

Exp. $\frac{18}{20}$ inch. *Hab.* Cayenne.

In the Collection of W. C. Hewitson.

The female has the spots and the outer half of the posterior wing on the upperside white.

Genus PTERYGOSPIDEA, *Wallengren.*

1. Pterygospidea Pteria.

Alis fuscis: anticis maculis decem albo-vitreis, posticis fascia macularum oblongarum nigrarum, angulo anali late albo: his infra
albis, maculis subcostalibus fuscis.

UPPERSIDE dark brown. Anterior wing with ten transparent spots : two in the cell, eight in a curved band beyond
the middle. Posterior wing crossed beyond the middle by a
band of oblong black spots : the outer margin from the
anal angle to the middle broadly white.

UNDERSIDE. Anterior wing as above, except that there
is a bifid white spot near the anal angle. Posterior wing
white, with the base and costal margin and some oblong
spots near it brown.

Exp. $1\frac{7}{10}$ inch. *Hab.* Philippines.

In the Collection of W. C. Hewitson.

Near to *P. trichoneura* of Felder.

2. Pterygospidea Permena.

Alis rufo-fuscis: anticis maculis octo albo-vitreis, tribus in medio
positis ; posticis fascia fulva, fasciaque macularum oblongarum
fuscarum.

UPPERSIDE dark brown. Anterior wing with eight

transparent spots : three in the centre (two of them large),
and five before the apex. Posterior wing crossed before the
middle by a band of yellow, and beyond the middle by a
band of oblong dark brown spots bordered outwardly with
paler colour.

UNDERSIDE as above, except that the posterior wing has
a white spot instead of the band.

Exp. $1\frac{7}{20}$ inch.   *Hab.* Macassar and Celebes.

In the Collection of W. C. Hewitson, from Mr. Wallace.

Near to the last and *P. Iapetus* of Cramer.

3. Pterygospidea Panthea.

Alis fuscis, lilacino tinctis, fasciis duabus nigris : infra rufo-fuscis.

UPPERSIDE dark brown, the basal half of both wings
tinted with lilac. Both wings crossed by two ill-defined
bands of dark brown ; the subbasal band short.

UNDERSIDE as above, except that it is rufous-brown.

Exp. $1\frac{7}{10}$ inch.   *Hab.* Amazon (Ega).

In the Collection of W. C. Hewitson, from Mr. Bates.

Belongs to the same group as *P. Iapetus.*

4. Pterygospidea Pekahia.

Alis utrinque griseo-fuscis, fascia pone medium fusca : anticis maculis octo albo-vitreis, tribus subcostalibus.

UPPERSIDE dark grey-brown. Both wings with the
outer margin and a transverse band beyond the middle dark
brown. Anterior wing with eight transparent white spots :
two in the middle, three in a line at a right angle from the
costal margin, and three before the apex.

UNDERSIDE as above.

Exp. $1\frac{4}{10}$ inch.   *Hab.* Venezuela.

In the Collection of W. C. Hewitson.

5. Pterygospidea leptogramma.

Alis fuscis : anticis maculis sex minutis semivitreis, fasciis duabus linearibus, venis maculisque turbinatis albis; posticis albis, basi grisea, apice fusco, venis maculisque lunularibus albis, margine exteriori griseo lunulis nigris.

UPPERSIDE dark rufous-brown. Anterior wing with six minute semitransparent white spots : one between the median nervules, three at the apex, and three nearer the outer margin below these : some small spots near the base, two linear broken bands near the middle, some of the nervures, and the outline of some conical spots beyond the middle white. Posterior wing white, with the base and two spots below the middle grey : part of the outer margin grey, marked by two black spots : the apex dark brown, marked by two conical outline spots of white.

UNDERSIDE as above, except that the anterior wing is without any of the white marks, and that the apex of the posterior wing and part of the outer margin (crossed by white nervures) are dark brown.

Exp. 1$\frac{6}{10}$ inch. *Hab.* Philippines.

In the Collection of W. C. Hewitson.

A beautiful species, most like *P. Pygela* in colour, but of very different form.

6. Pterygospidea Pygela.

Alis fuscis, basi fasciisque duabus albis; posticis margine exteriori sinuato late albo, fascia submarginali grisea : his infra albis, basi grisea, maculis subcostalibus griseo-fuscis.

UPPERSIDE dark brown. Both wings white at the base, both crossed by two bands of white : the first before the middle, nearly straight; the second beyond the middle, scarcely visible on the anterior wing, except near its inner margin, much curved on the posterior wing. Anterior wing with an indistinct submarginal band of paler brown. Posterior wing with the outer margin sinuated, broadly white, traversed by a band of brown.

UNDERSIDE. Anterior wing as above, but paler, the white bands less distinct. Posterior wing white, except the base, which is grey : a black spot near the base, some spots on the costal margin, and a spot near the anal angle brown.

Exp. 1$\frac{3}{10}$ inch. *Hab.* Borneo and Malacca.

In the Collection of W. C. Hewitson, from Mr. Wallace.

Belongs to the same group as *P. Sura* of Moore (*P. Helias,* Felder), and, though of very different form, is much like the last-described in colour.

7. Pterygospidea Phagesia.

Alis rufis : anticis angulo anali sinuato, maculis quatuor albovitreis, fasciaque lata fusca ; posticis fascia macularum minutarum apiceque fuscis, margine exteriori albo : his infra cæruleis.

UPPERSIDE rufous-brown. Anterior wing sinuated at the anal angle, with four central transparent spots : a broad transverse band beyond the middle, a linear band towards the apex, and a spot at the anal angle dark brown. Posterior wing with the apex, two spots on the costal margin, and a band of four minute spots beyond the middle dark brown : irrorated with grey towards the outer margin, which is white.

UNDERSIDE. Anterior wing rufous-brown, without the band and anal spot. Posterior wing blue, with the costal and outer margins rufous : the small black spots as above.

Exp. 1$\frac{3}{10}$ inch. *Hab.* Pará.

In the Collection of W. C. Hewitson.

Belongs to the same group as *P. Sura* of Moore, and is nearly allied to it.

Genus ÆTHILLA, *Hewitson*.

Head large. Body robust, short. Palpi with the third joint short. Antennæ rather long, the club slightly thicker at the bend, and tapering to a fine point somewhat as in *Eudamus,* but not so much bent. The outer margin of both wings taken together not much out of a straight line. Anterior wing with the apex much pointed; the cell long and narrow, the branches from the median nervure equidistant. The cell of the posterior wing half the length of the wing closed in a straight line from the third median nervule. Hind legs with four spurs, and a tuft of long hair from the base of the tibiæ.

This genus will come near to *Erycides.*

Æthilla Eleusinia.

Alis fuscis: anticis fasciis duabus nigris; posticis macula fasciaque obscuris, nigris, ciliis albis.

UPPERSIDE dark brown. Anterior wing crossed by two bands of darker brown. Posterior wing with a spot in the cell and a band below the middle very indistinct, the fringe white.

UNDERSIDE as above, except that it is without the bands and has the margins paler.

Exp. $2\frac{2}{10}$ inch. *Hab.* Quito.

In the Collection of W. C. Hewitson.

Genus CÆCINA, *Hewitson*.

Head small. Palpi with the last joint slightly projecting above the hair which clothes the lower part. Antennæ slender, half as long as the wing: the club slender, long, and pointed (not so much bent as in *Eudamus*). Body much shorter than the wings. Anterior wing with the costal margin irregularly arched, the apex truncated, the middle of the outer margin sinuated, the inner margin projecting near its base, and polished underneath, to cover a tuft of hair on the posterior wing : the cell long and narrow, closed obliquely ; the first branch of the median nervure distant from the rest. Posterior wing with the cell half the length of the wing closed in a straight line from the base of the second median nervule. Hind legs with four spurs.

This genus will rank near to *Eudamus*.

1. Cæcina Calathana.

Alis rufo-fuscis, macula cellulari fasciaque fuscis : posticis angulo anali ciliisque aurantiaco-fulvis : his infra margine exteriori late flavo.

UPPERSIDE rufous-brown. Both wings with a spot in the cell and a band of spots beyond the middle dark brown, indistinct. Posterior wing with the anal angle and the fringe orange-yellow.

UNDERSIDE as above, except that the outer margin, as well as the anal angle (apex excepted), is broadly yellow.

Exp. $2\frac{2}{10}$ inch. *Hab.* New Granada.

In the Collection of W. C. Hewitson.

Especially interesting from its great resemblance (except in shape) to *Eudamus Anaphus*.

2. Cæcina Compusa.

Alis rufis, macula cellulari fasciaque rufo-fuscis.

UPPERSIDE rufous. Both wings with a spot in the cell and a band of spots beyond the middle rufous-brown, indistinct.

UNDERSIDE as above, except that it is of a dull grey-brown.

Exp. $1\frac{17}{20}$ inch. *Hab.* Amazon.

In the Collection of W. C. Hewitson.

DESCRIPTIONS

OF

SOME NEW SPECIES

OF

LYCÆNIDÆ.

BY

W. C. HEWITSON.

LONDON:

JOHN VAN VOORST, 1 PATERNOSTER ROW.

June 1, 1868.

PREFACE.

WERE I aware that any entomologist was engaged in a monograph of any particular group of butterflies, I should consider that I merely performed an act of common courtesy in avoiding the said group until he had done with it. An entomologist, knowing that I am and have been for some time engaged in a monograph of the Lycænidæ, has, fortunately for me, given me notice that he is about to describe all those species in his possession. It is therefore in self-defence alone that I have been driven, greatly against my wish, to publish the following descriptions of species, many of which will, I hope, be figured and published in the present year.

What I have stated in speaking of the Hesperidæ I may repeat here, that " descriptions alone are utterly inadequate." The same synopsis will apply to a score of species, and, however minute, will not enable any one, with anything like certainty, to discriminate the difference without a figure to show the relative position of the band, and each spot in it, which crosses the posterior wing.

W. C. HEWITSON.

Oatlands, May 14th, 1868.

LYCÆNIDÆ.

Genus THECLA.

1. Thecla Thabena.

UPPERSIDE. *Male.*—Brilliant morpho-blue. The outer margins dark brown, broad at the apex of the anterior wing which has a large brown discal spot.

UNDERSIDE grey-white or stone-colour, tinted with lilac. Both wings crossed beyond the middle by two rufous-brown bands, the inner band bordered inwardly with orange, outwardly with white. Posterior wing with two tails; a round black spot on the costal margin at the commencement of the inner band: the anal angle broadly orange-yellow, marked by two black spots.

Exp. $\frac{19}{20}$ inch. *Hab.* Amazon.

In the Collection of W. C. Hewitson.

2. Thecla Temesa.

UPPERSIDE. *Male.*—Purple, the margins dark brown, narrow. Anterior wing with an oval discal brown spot. Posterior wing with two tails.

UNDERSIDE as in the last described.

Exp. 1 inch. *Hab.* Amazon and Cayenne.

In the Collection of W. C. Hewitson.

3. Thecla Talayra.

UPPERSIDE. *Male.*—Brilliant morpho-blue. The margins

Published June 1, 1868.

dark brown, broad at the apex and part of the outer margin of the anterior wing; the discal spot small and indistinct.

UNDERSIDE white. Both wings crossed beyond the middle by two transverse bands, the inner band rufous, commencing on the costal margin of the posterior wing by a round spot, and deeply arched towards the inner margin; the outer band brown, undulated on the posterior wing. Posterior wing with two tails. Anal angle with two rufous-orange spots, each marked with dark brown.

Exp. $\frac{19}{20}$ inch.   *Hab.* Rio de Janeiro.

In the Collection of W. C. Hewitson.

4. Thecla Terentia.

UPPERSIDE. *Female.*—Brown, darker at the outer margins, slightly tinted with lilac near the base. Posterior wing with a submarginal line of white.

UNDERSIDE grey-brown. Both wings crossed at and beyond the middle by two pale yellow bands: the inner band broad as it approaches the inner margin of the anterior wing, zigzag towards the inner margin of the posterior wing; the outer band of the posterior wing short. Anterior wing with a third band near the outer margin from the middle to the anal angle. Posterior wing with two tails, the outer margin very broadly orange-yellow marked by the two anal black spots and several submarginal spots of brown.

Exp. $1\frac{1}{20}$ inch.   *Hab.* Amazon.

In the Collections of H. W. Bates and W. C. Hewitson.

5. Thecla Tegæa.

UPPERSIDE. *Male.*—Rufous-brown. Anterior wing with the discal spot dark brown, oval, bordered with darker brown than the rest of the wing; an orange spot near the anal angle. Posterior wing with the outer margin broadly orange.

UNDERSIDE pale rufous-grey. Both wings crossed beyond the middle by a band of dark brown spots, bordered outwardly with white (broadly white near the inner margin of the posterior wing), commencing on the costal margin of the posterior wing by a round black spot; the anal angle orange, extending near the outer margin to beyond the middle; some submarginal brown spots, bordered on both sides with white.

Exp. $1\frac{3}{10}$ inch.

In the Collection of W. C. Hewitson.

6. Thecla Tarania.

UPPERSIDE. *Female.*—Rufous-brown. Posterior wing with two tails: the anal angle broadly orange.

UNDERSIDE paler, rufous. Anterior wing with two or three indistinct spots beyond the middle. Posterior wing crossed beyond the middle by two bands of white spots, the inner band bordered above with black and broadly by orange; the outer band bordered below with the same colours; a submarginal line of white.

Exp. $1\frac{1}{10}$ inch. *Hab.* Minas Geraes.

In the Collections of W. W. Saunders and W. C. Hewitson.

7. Thecla Teucria.

UPPERSIDE. *Female.*—Dark brown, with two small white spots and a line of white at the anal angle of the posterior wing.

UNDERSIDE grey-green. Anterior wing crossed beyond the middle by a band of white, bordered inwardly with brown, and by a submarginal band of the same colour from the anal angle to the middle. Posterior wing with two tails; crossed at the middle by a band of white spots: the apex (which is marked by a white spot) and the anal angle (which is irrorated with grey and marked by two black spots) very broadly brick-red, the space between them and two conical outline spots white: a submarginal band of white; the margin black.

Exp. $1\frac{1}{10}$ inch. *Hab.* Amazon.

In the Collections of W. W. Saunders and W. C. Hewitson.

8. Thecla tegula.

UPPERSIDE. *Male.*—Dark grey-brown. Anterior wing with an unusually long discal spot. Posterior wing with some grey lunular spots near the anal angle.

UNDERSIDE rufous-grey. Both wings crossed beyond the middle by a band of white, broken into lunular spots on the posterior wing. Anterior wing with some submarginal brown spots, bordered on both sides with white. Posterior wing with two tails : a white spot on the middle of the costal margin : the anal angle (which is irrorated with white and marked by two black spots) and the apex (which is bordered on both sides with white) brick-red : the space between them irrorated with white.

Exp. $1\frac{3}{10}$ inch. *Hab.* Amazon.

In the Collection of H. W. Bates.

9. Thecla Teatea.

UPPERSIDE. *Female.*—Rufous-brown, tinted with grey near the base. Posterior wing with two tails and an anal orange spot.

UNDERSIDE rufous. Both wings crossed at and beyond the middle by two bands of white : the inner band, which forms a W on the posterior wing, is bordered inwardly with black : the outer band, which is bordered outwardly with brown, is divided into spots, and nearer the other band on the posterior wing than it is on the anterior wing. Posterior wing with two black spots at the anal angle crowned with orange : a submarginal line of white : the margin black.

Exp. $1\frac{1}{10}$ inch. *Hab.* Amazon.

In the Collection of H. W. Bates.

10. Thecla Telea.

UPPERSIDE. *Male.*—Brilliant lilac-blue : the margins dark brown, narrow. Posterior wing with two tails.

UNDERSIDE bright green, with the fringe rufous-brown. Both wings crossed beyond the middle by an indistinct band of paler colour, silvery white where it takes the form of a W on the posterior wing, and bordered inwardly with red-brown : the anal angle broadly brick-red, bordered above and below with silvery white.

Exp. $\frac{8}{10}$ inch. *Hab.* Amazon.

In the Collection of W. C. Hewitson.

11. Thecla Ocrida.

UPPERSIDE. *Female.*—Dark grey-brown. Posterior wing with two tails and a submarginal white line.

UNDERSIDE grey-brown, clouded with dark brown in the middle. Both wings crossed beyond the middle by a band of dark brown, paler on its outer border; both with two indistinct submarginal brown bands. Anterior wing with a spot of yellow at the anal angle. Posterior wing with the outer margin broadly yellow, with the usual two black spots and some paler submarginal spots of brown.

Exp. $1\frac{3}{10}$ inch. *Hab.* Amazon.

In the Collection of W. C. Hewitson.

12. Thecla Ocrisia.

UPPERSIDE. *Male.*—Dark grey-brown. Anterior wing with the basal half smooth : the discal spot brown, round, and near the base. Posterior wing with the outer half except the apex cerulean blue, with a submarginal series of lunular spots.

UNDERSIDE dark brown. The outer margins of both wings marked with lunular brown spots, bordered with dull white. Anterior wing crossed beyond the middle by two dark-brown bands, the inner band bordered outwardly with dull white. Posterior wing marked near the centre by several indistinct irregular lunular spots of pale colour : a submarginal band of pale spots : a black spot between the tails, crowned with orange.

near the inner margin. Posterior wing with a long tail: crossed by three brown spots, two of which form a band below the middle.

UNDERSIDE as above, except that the posterior wing has a submarginal pale rufous band.

Exp. 1$\frac{6}{10}$ inch. *Hab.* Nicaragua.

In the Collection of W. C. Hewitson.

7. Eudamus Auginus.

Alis fuscis : anticis maculis vitreis : posticis infra macula lineari flava prope caudam posita : corpore viridi.

UPPERSIDE dark brown, the body green. Anterior wing with six transparent white spots : three in the form of a triangle in the centre, and three before the apex. Posterior wing with a broad dark brown tail.

UNDERSIDE as above, except that the posterior wing is glossed with green near the base, and has a linear pale-yellow spot near the base of the tail.

Exp. 1$\frac{7}{20}$ inch. *Hab.* Amazon.

In the Collection of W. C. Hewitson.

Very closely allied to the last, from which it differs chiefly in the pale linear spot of the underside. Specimens vary much in the relative length of the tail.

8. Eudamus Otriades.

Alis utrinque nigro-fuscis : posticis infra maculis duabus analibus parvis albis.

UPPERSIDE dark spotless brown, paler at the outer margins.

UNDERSIDE as above, except that there are two small white spots near the anal angle.

Exp. 1$\frac{8}{10}$ inch. *Hab.* Amazon.

In the Collection of W. C. Hewitson.

This species bears a very remarkable resemblance to an

Ismene in my Collection, which, though probably only a variety of *Goniloba Badra* of Moore, has not yet been described. This may be only a variety of the last described, *E. Auginus*, which seems to be a very variable species.

9. Eudamus obscurus.

Alis fuscis immaculatis: anticis infra macula apicali fusca: posticis fasciis duabus macularibus fuscis.

UPPERSIDE dark brown. Anterior wing with two very minute obscure transparent spots before the apex. Posterior wing with a short broad tail.

UNDERSIDE dark brown. Anterior wing as above, except that it is paler at the apex and outer margin, with a triangular dark brown spot near the apex: the inner margin pale rufous. Posterior wing sparingly irrorated with paler colour: two transverse bands of spots and the tail dark brown.

Exp. 1½ inch.

In the Collection of Dr. Boisduval.

10. Eudamus Aziris.

Alis rufo-fuscis: anticis maculis novem parvis vitreis: infra albo nigroque variatis: anticis basi ferruginea: posticis fascia maculisque nigris.

UPPERSIDE rufous-brown: the fringe alternately black and white. Anterior wing with nine transparent spots placed in circular form: four in a central band, two outside of these, and three (one apart from the other two) before the apex. Posterior wing with the anal angle protruded.

UNDERSIDE beautifully variegated with rufous-brown, grey, and black. Anterior wing with the base rufous: a white spot at the middle of the costal margin: the outer margin black. Posterior wing with a spot at the base, a margins, brilliant morpho-blue. Posterior wing with two tails, and a line of white above them.

UNDERSIDE pale grey, or stone-colour. Both wings with a brown line at the end of the cell: both crossed at the middle by a dark brown band bordered outwardly with white: both with a submarginal band of indistinct lunular brown spots : the lobe and spot between the tails black, broadly bordered above with orange.

Exp. $\frac{17}{20}$ inch. *Hab.* Amazon.

In the Collection of W. W. Saunders.

18. Thecla Gargara.

UPPERSIDE. *Female.*—Dark brown. Anterior wing with the base and inner margin blue. Posterior wing with two tails : the basal half blue.

UNDERSIDE pale grey, or stone-colour. Anterior wing crossed beyond the middle by an indistinct brown band: the wing beyond it rufous-brown. Posterior wing crossed at the middle by a dark brown band, and nearer the outer margin by a paler brown band: the space between the bands lilac-white : the lobe black, bordered above with yellow, the black spot between the tails crowned with orange, which is bordered above by yellow, below with grey.

Exp. 1 inch. *Hab.* Amazon.

In the Collection of H. W. Bates.

19. Thecla Ledæa.

UPPERSIDE. *Male.*—Anterior wing dark brown, with the basal third blue. Posterior wing with two tails : blue, with the costal margin rufous-brown, broad : the outer margin dark brown, narrow.

UNDERSIDE pale stone-colour, tinted with yellow. Both wings crossed beyond the middle by a band of rufous-brown bordered outwardly with white, commencing on the costal margin of the posterior wing by a single spot. Anterior wing with a short band of brown spots at the anal angle. Posterior wing with a submarginal band of lunular brown spots : the lobe black and white, bordered above with yellow : the black spot between the tails crowned with orange, which is bordered above with yellow.

Exp. $1\frac{1}{20}$ inch. *Hab.* Amazon.

In the Collection of H. W. Bates.

20. Thecla Gnosia.

UPPERSIDE rufous-brown : grey near the base of both wings. Posterior wing with one tail : blue from the median nervure to the inner margin : a submarginal line of white : the margin black : the fringe dull white.

UNDERSIDE pale stone-colour. Both wings crossed by a band of dark brown, bordered outwardly with white, the inner border rufous : both with a submarginal band of lunular brown spots bordered on both sides with white : the anal lobe and the black spot crowned with orange.

Exp. $\frac{8}{10}$ inch.

In the Collection of W. C. Hewitson.

21. Thecla Lebena.

UPPERSIDE. *Male.*—Brilliant violet-blue. Anterior wing with the apical half dark brown : the discal spot beyond the middle, red-brown. Posterior wing with two tails, the outer margin dark brown, narrow.

UNDERSIDE glossy-green. Both wings crossed beyond the middle by a band of brown, bordered outwardly with white. Anterior wing with a large triangular dark brown spot where the wings meet. Posterior wing with the lobe and black spot between the tails crowned with scarlet, which is bordered above with black : the space between these dark brown, irrorated with white, and bordered above with brown, and again with white : a submarginal white line.

Exp. $1\frac{1}{10}$ inch. *Hab.* Cayenne.

In the Collections of W. W. Saunders and W. C. Hewitson.

UPPERSIDE dark brown. Anterior wing with nine transparent spots : four (the first bifid) in a central band, one
outside of these, and four (two apart from the other two and
each other) placed very obliquely before the apex. Posterior
wing lobed.

UNDERSIDE rufous-brown. Posterior wing crossed by a
central narrow band of white : the inner margin near the anal
angle white.

Exp. 2 inches. *Hab.* Amazon.

In the Collection of W. C. Hewitson.

Very near to *E. Asander,* but differs from it in the less
oblique position of the band of the anterior wing, and the
clearly defined narrower band of the posterior wing.

15. Eudamus Naxos.

Alis fuscis, basi cærulea, maculis vitreis : posticis infra macula centrali alba maculisque octo ochraceis.

UPPERSIDE dark brown with the base of both wings
glossy blue. Anterior wing with eight transparent white
spots : five forming a central narrow band (one minute and
outside the others) and three before the apex. Posterior
wing with three white spots on the fringe near the apex.

UNDERSIDE rufous-brown. Anterior wing with the band
of transparent spots bordered inwardly with white, broad at
the first and fourth spots : a spot of grey on the outer margin
below these : the apex rufous. Posterior wing with a white
central spot followed by eight pale rufous spots.

Exp. $2\frac{2}{10}$ inches. *Hab.* Brazil.

In the Collection of W. C. Hewitson.

Near to *E. Apastus* and *E. Fulgerator.*

16. Eudamus Elorus.

Alis fuscis, basi viridi-cærulea : anticis fascia fusca : infra fasciis
duabus fuscis margine exteriori late rufescenti-cinereo.

UPPERSIDE rufous-brown, the base blue. Anterior wing crossed by two bands of darker brown.

UNDERSIDE rufous. Both wings crossed by two bands of dark brown: the outer band broad and succeeded by a broad marginal band of rufous-grey.

Exp. $2\frac{1}{10}$ inches.

In the Collection of W. C. Hewitson.

Near to *E. Anaphus*.

17. Eudamus Bryaxis.

Alis fuscis: anticis maculis vitreis: posticis ochraceis: his infra maculis duabus ad basin fasciisque duabus nigris: maculis submarginalibus albis.

UPPERSIDE dark brown: the base of the anterior wing and nearly the whole of the posterior wing covered with ochreous hair. Anterior wing with nine transparent white spots: four (the first bifid) forming a central band, one outside of these, and four before the apex. Posterior wing slightly lobed, dentated, the indentations white.

UNDERSIDE brown. Anterior wing as above, except that it has a rufous spot below the apical white spots and a submarginal row of spots of the same colour. Posterior wing with two spots near the base and two transverse irregular bands of dark brown: a submarginal band of brown spots bordered with white.

Exp. $2\frac{1}{10}$ inches. *Hab.* Guatemala.

In the Collection of W. C. Hewitson.

This bears a considerable resemblance to a tailed species (*E. Alcæus*), which is described above, from the same country.

18. Eudamus Enispe.

Alis rufo-fuscis: anticis maculis septem vitreis, quatuor in fascia obliqua, duabus prope apicem minutissimis: infra cinereo irroratis, lineis duabus transversis.

broad band near the base, and a band at the middle (which is marked by several small white spots) dark brown : two sub-anal bands of black and a submarginal line of white at the base of the tails.

Exp. $1\frac{2}{10}$ inch. *Hab.* Amazon.

In the Collection of H. W. Bates.

27. Thecla Badaca.

UPPERSIDE. *Male.*—Rufous-brown, tinted with grey on the posterior wing.

UNDERSIDE rufous. Both wings crossed beyond the middle by a band of dark brown, bordered inwardly with scarlet, and on the posterior wing outwardly with white. Anterior wing with a submarginal band of brown. Posterior wing with two tails : a submarginal undulated brown band, bordered above and below with paler colour ; the space between the bands darker brown : the lobe and black spot bordered above with scarlet.

Exp. $1\frac{1}{20}$ inch. *Hab.* Brazil.

In the Collection of W. C. Hewitson.

28. Thecla Biblia.

UPPERSIDE. *Male.*—Dark brown, with the fringe rufous.

UNDERSIDE green glossed with blue : a brown spot crowned with white at the anal angle of the posterior wing.

Exp. $\frac{8}{10}$ inch. *Hab.* Amazon.

In the Collection of H. W. Bates.

29. Thecla Blenina.

UPPERSIDE. *Male.*—Ochreous, tinted with orange. Anterior wing with the costal and outer margins broadly brown. Posterior wing with two tails : the outer margin dark brown, narrow.

UNDERSIDE green. Both wings crossed beyond the middle by a band of white, divided into spots on the terior wing; curved on the posterior wing from the costal

margin to the middle, where it forms two unusually acute
V-like angles : a subapical series of four black spots bordered
with white : the space between them and the tails irrorated
with white : the lobe black : a submarginal line of white :
the fringe silvery white.

Exp. $1\frac{1}{10}$ inch. *Hab.* Mexico.

In the Collection of W. C. Hewitson.

30. Thecla Bebrycia.

UPPERSIDE. *Male.*—Dark grey-brown. Anterior wing
with a dark brown discal spot within the cell. Posterior
wing with one tail : a conspicuous black spot crowned with
orange at the base of the tail, the lobe rufous, the space
between them brown, all bordered below with white : the
fringe white.

UNDERSIDE rufous-grey or stone-colour*, darker and
tinted with blue on the posterior wing. Both wings crossed
beyond the middle by a band of rufous-orange, slightly
bordered outwardly with black, and more distinctly with white.
Posterior wing with the lobe and the spot at the base of the
tail, and half of the space between them, black, bordered
above with orange : a submarginal line of white : the margin
black below these spots.

Exp. $1\frac{3}{10}$ inch. *Hab.* Mexico.

In the Collection of W. C. Hewitson.

31. Thecla Brescia.

UPPERSIDE. *Male.*—Blue. Anterior wing with the
discal spot small, round, pale brown, placed beyond the cell :
the costal and outer margins brown. Posterior wing with
two tails : costal and inner margins broadly rufous-brown :
the outer margin narrow, black : the lobe orange : a small spot
of brown between the tails.

UNDERSIDE grey or stone-colour, tinted with lilac. Both

---

* This colour, so frequent in this group of Butterflies, would perhaps
be best described as drab.

23. Eudamus Entellus.

Alis fuscis: anticis maculis novem vitreis: posticis macula rufa, his
infra maculis octo flavis.

UPPERSIDE dark brown. Anterior wing with nine transparent spots : four in the centre, two of which are large, two
minute, and five before the apex, two of which are under the
usual apical spots. Posterior wing with a small central
rufous spot.

UNDERSIDE as above, except that the posterior wing is
marked by eight yellow spots.

Exp. $2\frac{2}{10}$ inches. *Hab.* Java.

In the Collection of Dr. Boisduval.

24. Eudamus Phanæus.

Alis rufis: anticis maculis vitreis : posticis utrinque macula centrali
maculisque fuscis in semicirculum positis.

UPPERSIDE rufous. Anterior wing with eight transparent spots : three in the middle large, two below these minute and bordered with black, and three unusually large before the apex. Posterior wing with a central spot and a
semicircular band of spots below it black.

UNDERSIDE as above, except that the black spots of the
posterior wing are more obscurely marked.

Exp. $2\frac{1}{2}$ inches. *Hab.* Sarawak.

In the Collection of W. C. Hewitson, from Mr. Wallace.

25. Eudamus Phaselis.

Alis ochraceo-rufis: anticis maculis novem vitreis, tribus in triangulum pone medium, quinque sub apicem positis: posticis maculis
sex fuscis, infra tribus aliis ochraceis.

UPPERSIDE ochreous-brown. Anterior wing with nine
transparent spots : three in the middle (one of which is
broadly bordered with brown, the other two deeply sinuated),

one below these (which is small and bordered with black), three, as usual, before the apex, and two below them. Posterior wing with six dark brown spots : one in the centre and five forming a semicircular band below it.

UNDERSIDE as above, except that the posterior wing has the spots which are brown on the upperside pale yellow, with the addition of three more, one of which is near the addominal fold and two near the costal margin, making the semicircular band more complete.

Exp. $2\frac{6}{10}$ inches. *Hab.* Brazil.

In the Collection of Dr. Boisduval.

26. Eudamus Pherenice.

Alis anticis fuscis, maculis undecim vitreis: posticis angularibus, rufis, fasciis duabus fuscis : his infra obscure ochraceis, margine exteriori late lilacino-fuscis.

UPPERSIDE. Anterior wing dark brown, with eleven transparent spots : four in a broken band at the middle, one outside of these, and two small ones before the apical spots, which are four and of unequal size. Posterior wing angular, rufous, crossed by two dark brown bands.

UNDERSIDE. Anterior wing as above, except that it is tinted with lilac near the outer margin. Posterior wing with the bands as above, the basal half ochreous, the outer margin broadly lilac-brown.

Exp. $2\frac{7}{10}$ inches. *Hab.* Brazil.

In the Collection of W. C. Hewitson.

A beautiful species, with a general resemblance to *H. Santhilarius* of Latreille.

27. Eudamus Gonatas.

Alis rufo-fuscis : anticis margine externo reflexo, maculis sex vitreis separatim positis : posticis punctis tribus vitreis : his infra punctis vitreis ut supra, necnon punctis quatuor albis maculisque sex fuscis.

spots of scarlet near the base and by several spots of silver-green and white, three near the base of the costal margin, one below these, four on the inner margin, and eight at the anal angle.

Exp. 1⅒ inch.　*Hab.* Mexico.

In the Collection of W. C. Hewitson.

36. Thecla Carpophora.

UPPERSIDE. *Male.*—Blue : the margins dark brown, rather narrow. Anterior wing with an oblong discal spot of two colours, half in the cell, half beyond it : anal angle of the posterior wing (which has one tail) irrorated with white.

UNDERSIDE red-brown : the base of the costal margin of both wings crimson. Anterior wing with a minute white spot at the base, a line from the costal margin, and two spots below it between the median nervures white. Posterior wing with two or three minute spots at the base, a spot near the base of the costal margin, a circular spot, four spots at the middle, two linear spots near the inner margin, a subanal band, two spots above the lobe, a line at the base of the tail, and part of the fringe white : the lobe and the usual spot black.

Exp. 1⁹⁄₂₀ inch.　*Hab.* Mexico.

In the Collection of W. C. Hewitson.

37. Thecla Trebula.

UPPERSIDE. *Male.*—Anterior wing rufous-brown. Posterior wing with two tails : cerulean blue : the apex rufous-brown : the anal angle with three black spots, bordered below with white.

UNDERSIDE orange-yellow. Anterior wing crossed beyond the middle by a slender rufous-brown band, bordered outwardly with dull white. Posterior wing crossed beyond the middle by a dark brown band, bordered outwardly with white, commencing on the costal margin by an isolated spot, deeply arched above the anal angle : the lobe black, crowned with crimson : two very large spots at the base of the tails crimson, each marked by a small spot of black : the space between them dark brown, irrorated with white, and crowned with white, with a crimson spot above it : all bordered below with white.

Exp. $\frac{9}{10}$ inch. *Hab.* Amazon (Ega).

In the Collection of H. W. Bates.

38. Thecla Cydrara.

UPPERSIDE. *Male.*—Anterior wing dark brown, the base and inner margin broadly blue : the discal spot (which is within the cell) dark brown, indistinct. Posterior wing with two tails : blue, with the costal and inner margins rufous-brown : the outer margin dark brown, narrow : the lobe brown, with a fringe of white.

UNDERSIDE white. Both wings with a submarginal band of rufous spots. Anterior wing with a large triangular rufous spot at the middle of the costal margin : the fringe rufous. Posterior wing with five subbasal brown spots : crossed at the middle by a band of rufous spots : the lobe black, very slightly bordered above with orange-yellow.

Exp. $1\frac{1}{20}$ inch. *Hab.* Amazon.

In the Collection of W. C. Hewitson.

39. Thecla Ufentina.

UPPERSIDE. *Male.*—Brilliant green-blue. Anterior wing with the costal and outer margins dark brown : the discal spot within the cell. Posterior wing with one tail : the apex and outer margin, which is narrow, dark brown.

UNDERSIDE. Anterior wing rufous, tinted with lilac : crossed at the middle by a band of white, and by a sub-marginal band of lunular white spots, bordered below with brown. Posterior wing with the base of the costal margin, a spot before its middle, a subbasal band of spots, a band of spots : crossed by two indistinct bands of dark brown spots. Posterior wing with a spot of brown before the middle followed by a band of spots of the same colour.

UNDERSIDE as above, except that it is dark rufous-brown with the bands and spots less distinct.

Exp. 1½ inch. *Hab.* Amazon.

In the Collection of W. C. Hewitson.

Will come in the group to which *P. Avitus* of Cramer (plate 354) belongs.

32. Eudamus Azines.

Alis rufo-fuscis : anticis maculis vitreis, duabus magnis centralibus : posticis utrinque macula fasciaque maculari fuscis : his infra dimidio interno flavo.

UPPERSIDE rufous-brown. Anterior wing with six transparent spots : two, which are large, in the centre. Posterior wing with a brown spot before the middle and a band of spots of the same colour.

UNDERSIDE as above, except that the basal half of the posterior wing is yellow.

Exp. 1$\frac{9}{20}$ inch. *Hab.* Amazon.

In the Collection of W. C. Hewitson.

Near to *P. Avitus* of Cramer, but differs from it in the position and size of the transparent spots.

33. Eudamus Penidas.

Alis rufis : anticis maculis minutis vitreis : posticis utrinque fasciis duabus obscuris.

UPPERSIDE rufous. Anterior wing with seven small transparent white spots : four in the middle, one of which is deeply sinuated, and two triangular. Posterior wing crossed by two obscure bands slightly darker than the rest of the wing.

UNDERSIDE as above, except that the posterior wing is darker towards the outer margin.

Exp. 1½ inch. *Hab.* Amazon (Santarem).

In the Collection of W. C. Hewitson, from Mr. Bates.

34. Eudamus Phrynicus.

Alis fuscis: anticis macula costali fasciaque vitrea albis: posticis productis, margine exteriori utrinque albo, infra latiori.

UPPERSIDE dark brown. Anterior wing with a minute white spot on the costal margin, and below it a transverse transparent band of white. Posterior wing very long, with the outer margin white.

UNDERSIDE as above, except that it is rufous-brown, that the spot on the costal margin is larger so as to form part of the transverse band, and that the posterior wing is crossed by two scarcely seen bands of brown and has the white of the outer margin broader.

Exp. 2 inches. *Hab.* Amazon (St. Paulo).

In the Collection of W. C. Hewitson, from Mr. Bates.

This species is near to *C. Zarex* of Hübner's 'Zutrage,' figs. 183, 184, but twice as large.

35. Eudamus Phœnice.

Alis fuscis: anticis maculis vitreis maculaque flava: posticis fasciis duabus macularibus flavis: alis infra basi aurantiaca: posticis fascia lata alba.

UPPERSIDE dark rufous-brown. Anterior wing with seven transparent pale yellow spots: two at the middle, two outside of these, and three before the apex: a pale yellow spot near the middle of the inner margin. Posterior wing crossed by two bands, each of three pale yellow spots.

UNDERSIDE rufous-brown tinted with lilac. Anterior wing with the transparent spots as above, and a band of the anterior wing becoming broader as it approaches the anal angle: the band of the posterior wing consisting of six spots, three large and red bordered with brown first and then with white, and three smaller spots, which are brown, bordered with white: both wings with a band of pale brown spots bordered above with white, near the outer margin. Posterior wing with a submarginal band of pale brown spots: the lobe and a large spot at the base of the tail scarlet, each marked by a black spot with a white line below them.

Exp. $1\frac{2}{10}$ inch. *Hab.* Amazon.

In the Collection of W. C. Hewitson.

44. Thecla Fabulla.

UPPERSIDE. *Male.*—Dark brown. Anterior wing blue at the base and inner margin: the discal spot within the cell, small and pale brown. Posterior wing with two tails, the centre below the middle blue.

UNDERSIDE pale grey or stone-colour. Anterior wing crossed beyond the middle by a nearly straight short rufous band, bordered outwardly first with dark brown and then with white: a submarginal band of pale brown. Posterior wing nearly white from the middle to the outer margin: crossed at the middle by an irregular band of six brick-red spots, bordered outwardly first with black and then with white, the first spot at the costal margin, large; the second (which is minute), the fourth (which is bifid), and the fifth form a regular curve, whilst the third is within the rest and nearer the base, the sixth triangular: a submarginal band of lunular brown spots: the lobe and the spot between the tails (which is marked by a small black spot) orange.

Exp. $\frac{17}{20}$ inch. *Hab.* Venezuela.

In the Collection of W. C. Hewitson.

45. Thecla Petilla.

UPPERSIDE. *Male.*—Dark brown. Anterior wing blue

from the base to the middle of the costal margin. Posterior wing with two tails : brilliant morpho-blue : the outer margin dark brown, narrow.

UNDERSIDE pale grey or stone-colour. Anterior wing crossed beyond the middle by a narrow rufous band bordered outwardly first with brown then with white, commencing on the costal margin by an isolated spot, the spot at the middle of the band projecting outwards more than the others : a sub-marginal band of brown spots bordered with white. Posterior wing crossed at the middle by seven blood-red spots, bordered outwardly with black and white : the first spot on the costal margin below the others, the second, the third (which is shorter than the other two), and fourth touching : a sub-marginal series of pale brown spots : the anal angle and a spot between the tails blood-red.

Exp. $1\frac{1}{10}$ inch. *Hab.* Amazon.

In the Collection of H. W. Bates.

46. Thecla Calchinia.

UPPERSIDE. *Male.*—Dark brown. Anterior wing with the inner margin from the base to beyond the middle, and the whole of the posterior wing (except the apex and outer margin, which are dark brown), bright blue. Anterior wing with a large, ill-defined dark brown discal spot beyond the cell. Posterior wing with two tails : the anal angle with two black spots, bordered below with white.

UNDERSIDE white. Both wings with two brown lines at the end of the cell : both crossed at the middle by a rufous band bordered on both sides with brown, narrow at its commencement on the costal margin of the anterior wing, broader below, commencing on the costal margin of the posterior wing by an isolated spot : both wings crossed by a submarginal band of pale grey-brown lunular spots. Posterior wing with the lobe black and white bordered above with orange : the black spot between the tails crowned with orange : the margin black.

Exp. $\frac{9}{10}$ inch. *Hab.* Amazons.

In the Collection of H. W. Bates.

47. Thecla Ceglusa.

UPPERSIDE. *Male.*—Bright blue. Anterior wing with the costal and outer margins and apex (where it is broad) dark brown : the discal spot small, rufous, beyond the cell. Posterior wing with two tails : the lobe rufous, bordered with black : the outer margin black, narrow.

UNDERSIDE pale grey or stone-colour. Both wings crossed by two submarginal bands of brown spots. Anterior wing crossed beyond the middle by a dark red-brown band. Posterior wing crossed before the middle by a band of five brick-red spots bordered with dark brown : the first, third, and fourth large, the second small, the fifth triangular : the lobe and usual spot black.

Exp. $\frac{19}{20}$ inch. *Hab.* Amazon.

In the Collection of W. C. Hewitson.

48. Thecla Bagrada.

UPPERSIDE. *Male.*—Dark brown. Anterior wing, with part of the inner margin from the base, and the whole of the posterior wing, except the margins, dull lilac-blue. Anterior wing with the discal spot large, of two parts, filling the cell.

UNDERSIDE rufous, tinted with lilac. Both wings crossed beyond the middle by a band of scarlet, bordered outwardly first with black and outside of this with white, straight on the anterior wing, broken on the posterior wing, and commencing on the costal margin by an isolated red spot bordered on both sides with black and white. Anterior wing with a submarginal band of brown. Posterior wing with two tails : clouded with brown beyond the band : the lobe black and white, bordered above with scarlet ; the spot between the tails scarlet, marked by a small black spot: a submarginal line of white.

Exp. $1\frac{3}{10}$ inch. *Hab.* Villa Nova.

In the Collection of the British Museum.

49. Thecla Picentia.

UPPERSIDE. *Female.*—Rufous-brown. Posterior wing with two tails: the lobe rufous: a submarginal line of white at the base of the tails.

UNDERSIDE rufous, pale, tinted with orange. Both wings crossed by a brick-red band, bordered outwardly with black and white. Anterior wing with the band broadest near the costal margin: a submarginal pale rufous band. Posterior wing with the band unusually broad, unbroken, clouded with rufous-brown outside: the lobe and usual spot black, crowned with orange, and clouded above with brown: an indistinct brown band near the outer margin, and a submarginal white line.

Exp. $\frac{19}{20}$ inch. *Hab.* Amazon.

In the Collection of H. W. Bates.

50. Thecla Centoripa.

UPPERSIDE. *Male.*—Anterior wing dark blue-brown. Posterior wing with two tails: brilliant lilac-blue, with the outer margins broadly dark brown.

UNDERSIDE rufous-brown, clouded with darker lilac-brown. Both wings with a linear spot at the end of the cell: both crossed at the middle by a band of dark brown, commencing on the costal margin of the posterior wing by a large square spot (not isolated): the angular part of the band near the inner margin bordered with white. Posterior wing with a submarginal double series of indistinct lines of paler colour: the lobe and usual spot with a rufous border above, the space between them dark brown, bordered below with white.

Exp. 1 inch. *Hab.* Amazon.

In the Collection of W. C. Hewitson.

51. Thecla Ecbatana.

UPPERSIDE. *Male.*—Dark red-brown. Anterior wing with the costal margin and the whole of the posterior wing (except the costal margin) pale cerulean-blue. Posterior wing with two tails : the outer margin black.

UNDERSIDE lilac-grey, darker at the base and beyond the bands : variegated with white near the outer margins. Both wings with a linear spot at the end of the cell : both crossed near the middle by a broad rufous-brown band, bordered outwardly with brown and white. Anterior wing with a submarginal band of pale rufous-brown. Posterior wing with a submarginal series of pale brown spots, bordered with white : the lobe and usual spot black, bordered above with orange : the outer margin black.

Exp. $\frac{19}{20}$ inch. *Hab.* Amazon.

In the Collections of W. W. Saunders and W. C. Hewitson.

52. Thecla Besidia.

UPPERSIDE. *Female.*—Rufous-brown : the base of the inner margin of the anterior wing and the posterior wing (except the apex) pale cerulean-blue. Posterior wing with two tails : the lobe and two spots at the base of the tails dark brown, bordered below with white.

UNDERSIDE rufous, tinted with lilac. Anterior wing crossed beyond the middle by a brick-red band, bordered outwardly with black and white : a submarginal brown band : the fringe rufous. Posterior wing with two tails : crossed at the middle by a broad band of blood-red spots, bordered outwardly with black and white : the first spot on the costal margin (which is a little below the rest, but not separated) bordered above also with black and white : the wing beyond the band clouded with lilac-brown : the apex and part of the outer margin white, marked by some pale brown spots : the lobe and spot between the tails black, bordered above with scarlet.

Exp. 1 inch. *Hab.* Amazon.

In the Collection of H. W. Bates.

53. Thecla Demonassa.

UPPERSIDE. *Male.*—Dark brown. Posterior wing with one tail : brilliant morpho-blue, with the anal angle dark brown : the lobe rufous.

UNDERSIDE ochreous, tinted with orange. Both wings with a white line at the end of the cell : both crossed near the middle by a broad brick-red band, bordered outwardly with brown and white : both with a short band of brown near the anal angle, bordered with white on the posterior wing.

Exp. $\frac{9}{10}$ inch. *Hab.* Venezuela and Amazon.

In the Collections of W. C. Hewitson and H. W. Bates.

54. Thecla Buphonia.

UPPERSIDE. *Male.*—Rufous-brown.

UNDERSIDE orange-yellow: the fringe brown. Both wings crossed near the middle by a broad rufous band, bordered on both sides with brown (bordered outwardly on the anterior wing below the median nervure by pale brown) : narrower on the posterior wing as it approaches the inner margin, where the W is bordered outwardly with white. Posterior wing with two tails : the lobe black, crowned with white : a band of brown above the anal angle bordered above with white : the space between this band and the W orange.

Exp. $\frac{17}{20}$ inch. *Hab.* Amazon.

In the Collection of W. C. Hewitson.

55. Thecla Alda.

UPPERSIDE. *Male.*—Lilac-blue. Anterior wing with the costal and outer margin broadly brown : the discal spot small, round, dark brown, beyond the cell. Posterior wing with two tails: the fringe near them brown and white.

UNDERSIDE grey or stone-colour. Both wings with a line at the end of the cell: both crossed near the middle by a band of brown, rufous above, white below, commencing on the costal margin of the posterior wing by an isolated spot: both with a submarginal line of white. Anterior wing with a submarginal band of brown. Posterior wing with some brown spots near the base, one larger than the rest near the costal margin, two in the middle of the wing, and one near the inner margin: an irregular broad submarginal band irrorated with brown and white: the lobe and usual spot black, crowned with orange.

Exp. $\frac{17}{20}$ inch. *Hab.* Amazon.

In the Collection of H. W. Bates.

56. Thecla Ziba.

UPPERSIDE. *Female.*—Rufous-brown: posterior wing with two tails: the lobe orange, the black spot between the tails crowned with orange: two spots of white outside of these, and a submarginal white line.

UNDERSIDE grey-white. Both wings with two submarginal bands of pale brown. Anterior wing crossed beyond the middle by a band of six orange spots bordered outwardly with brown and white: with below these, near the inner margin, two pale spots of the same colour. Posterior wing with two subbasal orange spots: crossed at the middle by a band of orange spots, commencing on the costal margin by an isolated spot bordered on both sides with brown and white, the second spot also single: the lobe and the usual black spot crowned with orange.

Exp. $1\frac{3}{10}$ inch.

In the Collection of W. C. Hewitson.

57. Thecla Lucena.

UPPERSIDE. *Male.*—Dark brown. Anterior wing with

the inner margin blue : the discal spot dark brown, within the cell. Posterior wing with two tails : cerulean blue (except the costal and inner margins, which are broadly brown), marked near the inner margin by spots of dark brown : the lobe rufous, crowned with white.

UNDERSIDE grey or stone-colour. Both wings with a submarginal band of brown spots, bordered on both sides with white. Anterior wing with a spot at the end of the cell, a band (beyond the middle) of six rufous spots bordered on both sides with brown and white, the fourth spot projecting beyond the rest. Posterior wing with a small subbasal brown spot : crossed by two bands of rufous spots bordered on both sides with brown : the third and fourth spots of the second band (which is at the middle of the wing) projecting below the rest, and bordered above by a brown spot which is traversed by the line at the end of the cell : the lobe and the usual spot black, bordered above with orange.

Exp. $1\frac{3}{20}$ inch. *Hab.* Venezuela.

In the Collection of W. C. Hewitson.

58. Thecla Oreala.

UPPERSIDE. *Male.*—Dark brown. Anterior wing lilac-blue from the base below the median nervure : the discal spot large, within the cell. Posterior wing lilac-blue, with two tails and two spots of black at their base.

UNDERSIDE grey or stone-colour. Both wings with a spot at the end of the cell (bifid on the posterior wing) ; both with a submarginal band of pale brown spots. Anterior wing crossed much below the middle by a band of six brown spots (not separate), bordered on both sides with brown, broadly bordered outwardly with white. Posterior wing with a small spot near the base : crossed before the middle by a band of spots (two of which are large), and at the middle by a second band of brown spots bordered on both sides with darker brown : the space between this band and the submarginal band white : the lobe and the usual spot black, crowned with orange.

Exp. 1½ inch. *Hab.* Bahia.

In the Collection of H. W. Bates.

59. Thecla Arola.

UPPERSIDE. *Male.*—Rufous-brown. The costal margin of the anterior wing, and the whole of the posterior wing, except the apex, pale lilac-blue. Posterior wing with two tails : two spots of brown, the lobe rufous.

UNDERSIDE grey-white. Both wings with a linear spot at the end of the cell : both crossed at the middle by a band of rufous-orange spots, the three lowest spots on the anterior wing single : the first two spots on the posterior wing separate : both wings with a submarginal band of lunular brown spots bordered above with white, both with the outer margin orange. Posterior wing with a subbasal band of four orange spots (one minute) : the lobe and usual black spot crowned with orange.

Exp. 1$\frac{7}{20}$ inch. *Hab.* Brazil.

In the Collection of Dr. Boisduval.

60. Thecla Thulia.

UPPERSIDE. *Female.*—Rufous-brown. Posterior wing with two tails : the lobe orange : the spot between the tails black, crowned with orange : a submarginal line of white.

UNDERSIDE grey-white. Anterior wing crossed beyond the middle by a twice-broken rufous-brown band, bordered outwardly with white : a very indistinct submarginal band of spots. Posterior wing with two rufous spots before the middle : crossed at the middle by a band of rufous spots bordered outwardly with brown, commencing at the costal margin by an isolated spot bordered on both sides with brown : the second spot also single, small, and within the rest : two submarginal bands of lunular white spots : the lobe and the spot between the tails black, crowned with orange.

Exp. $1\frac{3}{20}$ inch. *Hab.* Amazon.

In the Collection of H. W. Bates.

61. Thecla Asa.

UPPERSIDE. *Male.*—Lilac-blue. Anterior wing with more than the outer half dark brown. Posterior wing with two tails : the outer margin dark brown, narrow.

UNDERSIDE pale stone-colour. Both wings crossed near the middle by a rufous band, bordered outwardly with brown and white, placed obliquely and twice broken on the anterior wing, commencing on the posterior wing by a large isolated spot : both wings crossed beyond the middle by a band of white lunular spots, placed much out of line on the posterior wing, the spot nearest the inner margin bordered below with orange : both wings with a submarginal band of lunular white spots. Posterior wing—the lobe brown, bordered above with white and orange : the spot between the tails large, orange, marked with a black spot.

Exp. $\frac{8}{10}$ inch. *Hab.* Amazon.

In the Collection of H. W. Bates.

62. Thecla socia.

UPPERSIDE. *Male.*—Dark brown. Anterior wing with the inner margin from the base to beyond its middle cerulean-blue : the discal spot small, round, pale, within the cell. Posterior wing with one tail : cerulean blue, with the costal margin and apex brown.

UNDERSIDE rufous, tinted with carmine. Anterior wing crossed beyond the middle by a continuous carmine band, bordered outwardly with white : a submarginal band of red-brown spots. Posterior wing crossed at the middle by a continuous carmine band, bordered on both sides with white, projecting outwards in the form of a square spot, but not detached from the band : a broad submarginal band irrorated with white, brown, and carmine, commencing near the costal margin by a carmine spot : the lobe and usual spot carmine : a submarginal white line : the margin black.

Exp. $1\frac{3}{20}$ inch.　*Hab.* Brazil.

In the Collection of Dr. Boisduval.

63. Thecla Agra.

UPPERSIDE. *Male.*—Rufous-brown. Anterior wing with a dark brown discal spot. Posterior wing without tails : pale lilac-blue, with the costal margin brown : the outer margin and the usual spot dark brown : the fringe white.

UNDERSIDE. Anterior wing rufous, darker near the outer margin, where it is crossed by a band of white, triangular at the apex, forming a large spot at the anal angle. Posterior wing white, clouded with rufous-brown, a spot before the middle of the costal margin, a large triangular spot at the apex, and a large spot at the base of the inner margin all dark rufous-brown.

Exp. $\frac{9}{10}$ inch.　*Hab.* Amazon.

In the Collection of W. C. Hewitson.

This and some of the following species have much resemblance to the *Lycænæ.*

64. Thecla Hygela.

UPPERSIDE dull lilac-blue. Anterior wing with the costal and outer margins broadly brown : the discal spot dark brown, within the cell. Posterior wing with two tails : the apex and outer margin brown.

UNDERSIDE clouded and irrorated throughout with brown. Both wings with a submarginal brown line. Anterior wing crossed by two broad bands of dark brown, with a white spot between them. Posterior wing with two large spots near the base and a central band of brown : the spot between the tails rufous.

Exp. $\frac{8}{10}$ inch.

In the Collection of W. C. Hewitson.

65. Thecla Davara.

UPPERSIDE rufous-brown. Posterior wing with one tail : irrorated with pale blue : a submarginal series of brown spots, bordered with grey-white.

UNDERSIDE grey-white, irrorated with brown. Anterior wing with the basal half rufous : crossed beyond the middle by a broad band of brown and by a submarginal band which joins it before the anal angle. Posterior wing with the inner margin from the base and a broad band from the middle of the costal margin brown, united below the middle of the wing : the apex and two spots at the anal angle brown.

Exp. $\frac{9}{10}$ inch.
In the Collection of W. C. Hewitson.

66. Thecla Faunalia.

UPPERSIDE. *Male.*—Rufous-brown. Anterior wing with the discal spot large, dark brown, within the cell. Posterior wing with one tail : two dark brown spots at the anal angle bordered below with white : the margin black, the fringe white.

UNDERSIDE white, clouded with grey-brown. Anterior wing rufous to near the apex where it is crossed obliquely by an undulated band of dark brown and by two submarginal bands of brown spots. Posterior wing with the base, a band near it of six spots : a central band of brown spots bordered with darker brown the second and third spots projected below the rest : a submarginal band of brown spots : the caudal spot black.

Exp. $\frac{8}{10}$ inch. *Hab.* Amazon.
In the Collection of W. C. Hewitson.

67. Thecla Salona.

UPPERSIDE rufous-brown, grey at the base. Posterior

wing without tails : two dark brown spots at the anal angle, bordered below with white.

UNDERSIDE pale grey or stone-colour. Both wings crossed by two submarginal bands of pale brown spots bordered with white. Anterior wing crossed beyond the middle by a band of five rufous-brown spots, bordered outwardly with white. Posterior wing with two spots near the base, a linear spot at the end of the cell, and a band of dark brown spots at the middle all circled with white.: the lobe black : the spot near it large and black, crowned with orange.

Exp. $\frac{9}{10}$ inch. *Hab.* Venezuela.

In the Collection of W. C. Hewitson.

68. Thecla Fidentia.

UPPERSIDE. *Female.*—Dark brown. Anterior wing with the inner margin near the base cerulean blue. Posterior wing with two tails : cerulean blue : two brown spots at the anal angle bordered below with white.

UNDERSIDE. Anterior wing grey-brown, with a line at the end of the cell, a rufous band beyond the middle broken below the median nervure : the space between it and the outer margin white, traversed by a zigzag band of crimson. Posterior wing white, with some spots near the base, a double line at the end of the cell, a band of spots at the middle, a submarginal band of spots and the outer margin all carmine : the space between the bands irrorated with carmine.

Exp. $\frac{9}{10}$ inch. *Hab.* Venezuela.

In the Collection of W. C. Hewitson.

69. Thecla Limenia.

UPPERSIDE. *Male.*—Rufous-brown. Anterior wing

with a brown undefined discal spot. Posterior wing with one tail : some brown spots at the anal angle : the lobe rufous.

UNDERSIDE pale grey or stone-colour. Both wings with a line at the end of the cell : both crossed by a band of dark brown spots bordered outwardly with white, commencing on the posterior wing by a large oval black spot. Anterior wing with a submarginal band of brown spots. Posterior wing with two brown subbasal spots : two submarginal bands of pale brown, bordered inwardly with white : the lobe black, bordered above with white and orange : the spot near the base of the tail large, orange : the space between the spots brown, irrorated with blue.

Exp. 1 inch. *Hab.* Jamaica.

In the Collection of W. W. Saunders.

70. Thecla Lycimna.

UPPERSIDE. *Male.*—Metallic-blue, with the margins brown, the lobe projecting.

UNDERSIDE bright green. Posterior wing tailless : crossed beyond the middle by four or five distant white spots : a submarginal band of spots and the lobe red-brown.

Exp. $1\frac{3}{10}$ inch.

In the Collection of W. C. Hewitson.

71. Thecla Leucania.

UPPERSIDE. *Male.*—Dull grey-blue, with the margins brown, the lobe rufous.

UNDERSIDE pale green. Posterior wing with one tail : crossed by a submarginal band of white spots, bordered inwardly with red-brown : the lobe dark red-brown : the usual spot and the spot between them red-brown, irrorated with white.

Exp. $1\frac{2}{10}$ inch. *Hab.* Mexico.

In the Collection of W. C. Hewitson.

Differs from the last in having the white spots of the posterior wing much nearer to the outer margin.

72. Thecla longula.

UPPERSIDE. *Male.*—Brilliant morpho-blue, with the margins dark brown.

UNDERSIDE dull green, tinted with orange at the apex of the anterior wing. Posterior wing without tails : crossed beyond the middle by two bands of indistinct distant red-brown spots : a series of marginal red-brown spots, irrorated with white : the lobe red-brown.

Exp. $1\frac{1}{10}$ inch. *Hab.* Mexico.

In the Collection of W. C. Hewitson.

73. Thecla Remus.

UPPERSIDE. *Female.*—Dark brown. Both wings with the basal half dull blue-grey : the lobe broadly rufous.

UNDERSIDE green. Anterior wing crossed beyond the middle and near the costal margin by a band of three or four rufous spots. Posterior wing, with part of the costal margin, orange-rufous : the base, a band at the middle, two spots near the anal angle, and a series of lunular spots on the outer margin (which are irrorated with white) all red-brown.

Exp. $1\frac{3}{20}$ inch. *Hab.* Brazil.

In the Collection of Dr. Boisduval.

74. Thecla Cecina.

UPPERSIDE. *Male.*—Brilliant blue, tinted with green at the base. Anterior wing with the margins and nervures (which divide the blue into segments) dark brown : the discal spot small, pale, and within the cell. Posterior wing with two tails : the inner margin and apex brown : the lobe irrorated with green.

UNDERSIDE bright green : the margins red-brown. Pos-

terior wing crossed beyond the middle by a band of small
dark brown spots, one at the apex isolated, the rest towards the anal angle: the lobe and usual spot dark red-
brown.

Exp. $1\frac{5}{20}$ inch. *Hab.* Guatemala (Polochic valley).
In the Collection of Messrs. Salvin and Godman.

75. Thecla Sangala.

UPPERSIDE. *Male.*—Rufous-brown, pale and tinted
with grey at the base of the posterior wing. Anterior wing
with the costal margin orange. Posterior wing with two
tails: the lobe orange: the usual spot and the spot between
them dark brown, bordered above with orange: a submarginal line of white.

UNDERSIDE pale rufous-grey. Both wings crossed beyond the middle by a band of orange bordered outwardly
with white, the W very distinct: the lobe black and crowned
with white and orange: the spot between the tails large,
orange, marked by a black spot: between this spot and the
apex an indistinct rufous-brown band.

Exp. $1\frac{1}{10}$ inch. *Hab.* Venezuela.
In the Collection of W. C. Hewitson.

76. Thecla Quaderna.

UPPERSIDE dark brown: the fringe rufous-orange. Anterior wing with the inner margin from its base to its
middle, and the whole of the posterior wing (except the
apex, which is broadly brown) cerulean blue. Posterior
wing without tails: some submarginal brown spots.

UNDERSIDE pale grey or stone-colour. Both wings
crossed beyond the middle by a band of orange spots bordered outwardly with white, commencing on the costal
margin of the posterior wing by an isolated spot much
within the rest. Anterior wing with a small brown spot at

the middle of the inner margin.   Posterior wing with a sub-marginal band of orange spots.

Exp. 1 inch.   *Hab*. Mexico.

In the Collection of W. C. Hewitson.

EQUATORIAL LEPIDOPTERA

COLLECTED BY Mr. BUCKLEY.

DESCRIBED BY

W. C. HEWITSON.

PART I.

LONDON:

JOHN VAN VOORST, 1 PATERNOSTER ROW.

December 2, 1869.

PREFACE.

I do not, of course, compare the collection of Mr. Buckley with the perennial collections of Bates and Wallace, which increased by one-third the known butterflies; but I do not hesitate in saying, that during the twenty-five years in which I have been a student of these things, no such single collection (either for its perfection or extent) has been brought to Europe.

Mr. Buckley was only absent from England fourteen months; he had to cross the Andes from Guayaquil to reach his hunting-ground, had almost constant rain during his absence, and yet contrived to bring home with him 5000 butterflies, most of them as fresh and beautiful as if they had been reared from the caterpillars at home. I did not think it necessary, in describing the new species, to attach the exact locality to each, since they were all taken over a district less in extent than that of England: but to meet the wishes of others, who think differently, I have added a list of the species, with the precise locality of each. The furthest point reached by Mr. Buckley was St. Rosas, on the Napo river. He left Guayaquil on the 5th of July, 1868, and, after staying ten days at Riobamba and Baños, and nearly two months at St. Ines (a solitary hut), he reached Canelos on the 17th of October. From Canelos he went to Sarayaco, leaving it on the 30th of November for St. Rosas, staying on his way for a month at Curaray. He remained a very short time at St.

Rosas, returning again to Curaray and Sarayaco, from whence he made an excursion down the Rio Bobanaza to the mouth of the Rio Ratuno, spending several days upon the banks of that river. He was again, on his return journey, at Canelos, at St. Ines another month, stayed at Jorge twenty days, and reached Guayaquil on the 26th of June. Four genera are largely represented in this collection, as will be seen by the new species described; these are *Leptalis, Ithomia, Eresia,* and *Mesosemia.* It may be interesting to state that the *Morpho Phanodemus,* one of a race which usually fly so high that it is impossible to catch them, was passing near the ground, with the immoveable flight of a bird of prey, when it was knocked down by Mr. Buckley's hat, and that the only specimen he saw of the *Agrias Beatifica* was caught under a basket by a native boy.

I have described 145 new species, minus two in which I had been anticipated. I might have added many more, which would have been considered good by other Lepidopterists. In the *Hesperidæ* I have several other new species, but so obscure that I am unwilling to put them into print.

I have to regret the following errors. My *Eueides Acacetes* has been previously described by Mr. Bates under the name of *Lampeto.*

Herrich-Schäffer has divided my *Ithomia Lavinia,* proposing the name of *Vanilia* for figures 35 & 36. *Lavinia* will therefore stand for figure 34, and the name of *Mirza* cease.

Mr. Kirby proposes to call *Eresia Mylitta E. Bella,* my name having been used in *Melitæa.*

REMARKS ON AND DESCRIPTIONS OF

NEW SPECIES OF BUTTERFLIES

COLLECTED BY Mr. BUCKLEY

IN ECUADOR.

PAPILIONIDÆ.

PAPILIO.

In this genus the collection is not rich. It contains few species, the most interesting of which are:—
P. Zagreus. P. Columbus. P. Ctesias. P. Coristheus (P. Aristeus, Cram.) : my specimen agrees very well with Cramer's figure, but is as large as *P. xanthopleura* of Salvin.

There is one species only which I consider new, and this is remarkable for the white bands of both wings.

1. Papilio Lacydes.

UPPERSIDE. *Female.*—Dark brown : the outer margins marked by white lunular spots. Anterior wing crossed obliquely a little beyond the middle by a broad oblique band of white divided by the nervures into eight parts. Posterior wing crossed towards the outer margin by a curved band of white divided into six spots (two of which nearest to the apex are isolated) by the nervures.

UNDERSIDE precisely as above.

Exp. 4 inches.

Nearest to *P. Cyphotes* of G. R. Gray.

Published December 2, 1869.

PIERIDÆ.

The genus *Pieris* contains the following rare species in abundance :—

P. Cæsia of Lucas and *P. cinerea* which I have described but not yet figured.

In *Hesperocharis* there are two species of interest, *H. Nereis* of Felder, and *H. Hirlanda* (var. *Helvia*) in great beauty.

Of *Colias* there is a single representative.

Callidryas contains a female of *C. Cypris* (*Rurina*, Felder).

In *Terias* I have ventured to describe one species which I believe to be new. I must apologize for adding one more to the perplexing maze of descriptions with which we are already sufficiently puzzled.

2. Terias Ecuadora.

UPPERSIDE. *Female*.—White, tinted with yellow, chiefly at the base : the outer half of both wings black, beginning at the apex of the anterior wing (not touching the costal margin) and extending on its inner margin in an irregular line to the inner margin before the middle. Posterior wing angular. The inner border of the black margin commences at the apex, and curving upwards to the end of the cell curves downwards to the anal angle : a large spot of bright yellow on the costal margin.

UNDERSIDE. Anterior wing white, with the base and costal and outer margins yellow : a minute black spot at the end of the cell. Posterior wing yellow, with several small spots, a spot on the costal margin, and an oblique band crossing the discoidal nervures, all rufous.

Exp. $1\frac{7}{10}$ inch.

Near *T. Mexicana*, but with a much broader margin of black : *the costal margin of the anterior wing white to the apex.*

Euterpe contains several interesting species :—*E. Eurytele* in abundance; of *E. Tereas,* a variety without the white spots of the anterior wing; *E. Corcyra* of Felder; and two beautiful species, which are here described.

3. Euterpe Anaitis.

UPPERSIDE. *Female.*—Black. Both wings with a submarginal series of indistinct white spots scarcely visible on the posterior wing. Anterior wing with a white spot in the cell, and a transverse band near the middle which commences at the costal margin by four small spots and afterwards becomes very broad as it approaches the inner margin; it is divided by broad black nervures. Posterior wing with the basal half yellow (the base itself irrorated with brown), divided by black nervures.

UNDERSIDE red-brown: as above, except that the anterior wing has hastate rays of yellow from the outer margin, each with a large white lunular spot at its point, and that the posterior wing has the base dark brown marked by four white spots, a submarginal series of very large sagittate silvery-white and yellow spots, and a marginal series of triangular spots of yellow.

Exp. $2\frac{7}{10}$ inches.

4. Euterpe Ctemene.

UPPERSIDE white. Anterior wing with the base broadly brown, irrorated with white: the costal margin (which is marked by a bifid white spot at the end of the cell) and the apical third (which is traversed by a straight band of six white spots, and has its inner border straight) all dark brown. Posterior wing with the base irrorated with brown, the nervures at their base and towards the outer margin black: the outer margin spotted with brown.

UNDERSIDE red-brown. Anterior wing as above, except that there is a white and yellow spot near the apex, and rays of yellow from the outer margin between the nervures.

Posterior wing with two small spots at the base, a longitudinal line in the cell, a pair of minute spots at the end of the cell, and rays from the outer margin between the nervures, all yellow : *three rather large spots near the base,* and spots in pairs between the marginal rays, all lilac-white.

Exp. 2 inches.

In general resemblance like *E. Teutamis* of Hewitson.

In *Leptalis* the collection is of great value, and contains a large portion of the rarest species which have been hitherto figured or described. I did at first believe that I should have the pleasure of describing ten new species ; two of these, however, have been put together as the sexes of one species, and another has been previously described by me from the collection of Mr. Druce. I have added a list of all the species to show the extraordinary richness of the collection in these very rare things.

L. Orise. L. Larunda, *n. sp.* L. Amphione. L. Laia. L. Carthesis. L. Euryope. L. Lua, *n. sp.* L. Idonia, *n. sp.* L. Zaela. L. Melite. L. Mercenaria. L. Medora. L. Lysis, *n. sp.* L. Lelex, *n. sp.* L. Othoë. L. Zathoë. L. Leonora, *n. sp.* L. Lygdamis, *n. sp.* L. Avonia. L. Critomedia. L. Eumelia. L. Ithomia. L. Lysinoë. L. Theonoë. L. Teresa, *n. sp.* L. Nemesis. L. Nehemia.

5. Leptalis Larunda.

UPPERSIDE. *Male.*—Anterior wing black, with a large scarlet spot at the base intersected by three nervures, and very irregular in form : crossed before the middle by an irregular sexfid oblique band of pale yellow : a subapical band of four small oval yellow spots. Posterior wing with the base scarlet, the outer margin broadly dark brown, marked by a yellow spot, the costal margin white, polished.

UNDERSIDE. Anterior wing as above, except that the basal half (except the costal margin, which is dark brown) is white and polished, and that there is a yellow spot near the costal margin beyond the middle. Posterior wing with the basal half scarlét, followed by a transverse band of yellow marked by two black spots: the outer margin broadly dark brown, traversed by a submarginal band of small white spots, in pairs except near the apex.

Exp. 3 inches.

Nearly as large as *L. Orise*, but unlike any other species.

6. Leptalis Lua.

UPPERSIDE. *Male.*—Dark brown. Anterior wing with seven yellow spots: one before and below the middle, three in an oblique transverse band beyond the middle, and three smaller ones before the apex. Posterior wing crossed longitudinally by a broad quinquefid band of yellow: the costal margin broadly white, not polished, dentated near the apex.

UNDERSIDE. Anterior wing opaque white, not polished: the costal margin and apex yellow, the nervures brown. Posterior wing pale rufous-brown, with nine spots and the band as above, yellow: the outer margin irrorated with yellow.

Exp. $2\frac{3}{10}$ inches.

Unlike any other species: most like *L. Nemesis* on the upperside.

7. Leptalis Idonia.

UPPERSIDE. *Male.*—Dark brown. Anterior wing crossed obliquely by two bands of yellow spots: the first band at the middle with two spots the first of which is large and sinuate: the second band of three spots before the apex. Posterior wing crossed obliquely from the middle of the inner margin by a broad band of yellow divided into four parts by the nervures: the fourth part which is beyond the third median nervule, is marked on its outer border by a black spot: the costal margin polished where the wings meet.

UNDERSIDE. Anterior wing as above, except that it is

pale grey-brown and has the apex ochreous-yellow. Posterior wing clouded ochreous-yellow with the band as above but very indistinct.

Exp. $2\frac{2}{10}$ inches.

This species does not differ from *L. Arcadia* of Felder on the upperside, but is very different below.

8. Leptalis Lysis.

UPPERSIDE. *Male.*—Dark brown. Anterior wing oval, with a large white spot from the costal margin beyond its middle, and a smaller triangular spot, also white, on the inner margin. Posterior wing polished where it meets the anterior wing : crossed beyond the middle by a broad longitudinal band of white.

UNDERSIDE ochreous-yellow irrorated with brown. Anterior wing with the white spots as above. Posterior wing with the longitudinal band as above divided by the nervures into eight parts : the base of the costal margin and a spot near it yellow : a white spot near the costal margin before its middle.

Female like the male, except that the anterior wing is crossed on both sides by a broad white band, and that its base to this band and a large spot on the opposite margin are brown.

Exp. $1\frac{8}{10}$ nch.

Like the next, near to *L. Zathoë* and *L. Othoë.*

9. Leptalis Lelex.

UPPERSIDE. *Male.*—Anterior wing dark brown, with the inner margin angular : marked by four pale yellow spots : one (a large one) from the middle of the costal margin : the second, also large, fills the projecting angle of the inner margin : the other two (one scarcely visible) small, before the apex. Posterior wing yellow, polished where the wings meet : the outer margin from the apex to the middle dark brown, dentated inwardly.

UNDERSIDE pale yellow. Anterior wing slightly clouded with grey, polished where it meets the posterior wing : the spots as above though indistinct.

Exp. $1\frac{9}{10}$ inch.

Nearest to *L. Zathoë,* Hewitson.

10. Leptalis Leonora.

UPPERSIDE. *Male.*—Anterior wing black, with a line from the base, a spot on the middle of the costal margin, a spot below this, a large spot on the inner margin, and two small subapical spots all pale yellow. Posterior wing brown, darker at the outer margin : polished white where it meets the other wing : the space between the median nervure and the anal angle grey-blue.

UNDERSIDE. Anterior wing glossy lilac-white : the apex slightly irrorated with brown. Posterior wing irrorated with brown and yellow : three spots near the costal margin before its middle and an irregular band of eight spots at the middle (one within the cell) all white : the nervures and spots where they touch the outer margin dark brown : the outer margin yellow.

Female.—Dark brown : a large space from the inner margin to the middle of the wing, an oblong spot from the middle of the costal margin, and two subapical spots all yellow-white. Posterior wing with the basal half white. On the underside the anterior wing is as above, except that the apex is irrorated with yellow and brown. The posterior wing nearly as in the male.

Exp. $2\frac{2}{10}$ inches.

A variety of the female has the outer margin of the posterior wing white from the middle to the anal angle.

11. Leptalis Lygdamis.

UPPERSIDE. *Male.*—Dark brown. Anterior wing with a quadrate quinquefid spot at the middle of the costal margin, a large bifid spot on the inner margin before its middle, and a minute spot on the costal margin beyond its middle all white. Posterior wing with the basal half (except the base itself, which is brown) white, slightly polished.

UNDERSIDE. Anterior wing grey-white, not polished : costal margin and apex brown marked by a series of white and yellow spots. Posterior wing dark rufous-brown, with four small spots near the base, a large spot within the cell, a transverse band of ten spots, and a submarginal band of eight spots all yellow.

Female.—White. Anterior wing with the costal margin broadly brown from the base to the middle : the apex very broadly brown dentated inwardly, and marked on the costal margin beyond the middle by a white spot. Posterior wing with the outer margin dark brown, of unequal breadth, and deeply indented inwardly. Underside as in the male, except that the lower spots of the transverse band and some of the submarginal spots are so much larger that they touch each other.

Exp. 2 inches.

12. Leptalis Teresa.

UPPERSIDE black. *Male.*—Anterior wing with a pale triangular spot at the base : crossed by two oblique bands, each of three white spots, the first band in the middle, its first two spots bifid : the second band before the apex, the first spot bifid. Posterior wing with its centre lilac-white, smeared with brown, divided by black nervures : a sub-apical white spot.

UNDERSIDE as above, except that the outer margin of the anterior wing and the whole of the posterior wing are dirty, obscure grey-brown.

Female.—Dark brown. Anterior wing crossed obliquely at the middle by a band of pale yellow, in-dented on its inner border, and terminating in a point below the middle of the wing : crossed before the apex by three small white spots : the inner margin yellow. Posterior wing yellow, with the outer margin broadly dark brown. On the underside the anterior wing is as above, except that the apex is grey : the posterior wing is grey-brown, with a spot on the costal margin, a band of nine spots at the middle, and a spot below these white : the outer margin is also irrorated with white.

Exp. $2\frac{3}{10}$ inches.

HELICONIDÆ.

In Ecuador Mr. Buckley seems to have reached the head-quarters of the *Heliconidæ* generally, but more especially of the genus *Ithomia*, not only capturing a number of new and remarkable species, but also many which we have received from the Amazon and from Bogota.

In the genus *Heliconia*, although four species only are described which are new, the collection contains several which have been hitherto very rare—amongst them *H. Cyrbia*, *H. notabilis* of Salvin (near to *H. Xenoclea*), and *H. Telesiphe*. Of the ever-varying *H. Thelxiope* there is one beautiful variety which, without the scarlet at the base of both wings, has the rays only of the posterior wing broad and vivid.

13. Heliconia Cythera.

UPPERSIDE. *Male.*—Black glossed with green-blue. Anterior wing crossed transversely beyond the middle by a quinquefid band of carmine and white : the outer margin with minute white spots. Posterior wing with the outer margin white, intersected at the end of the nervures by distinct black lines.

UNDERSIDE as above, except that the band of the anterior wing is paler, and that the posterior wing has the base of the costal margin, and a longitudinal band before the middle yellow.

Exp. $2\frac{8}{10}$ inches.

Very near to *H. Cyrbia*, but differs from it in having the anterior wing narrower, the outer margin spotted with white only (whilst *Cyrbia* has the fringe altogether white), and in having the white outer margin of the posterior wing broader, and not intersected by black lines between the nervures.

14. Heliconia Alithea.

UPPERSIDE dark brown, tinted with blue near the base of both wings. Anterior wing crossed at the middle by a broad irregular band of yellow, divided by black nervures into eight parts, increasing in size from that on the costal margin, which is bifid : a spot below these at the anal angle also yellow. Posterior wing with the outer margin broadly yellow, intersected by the nervures which are black, and divided on the inner border by black lines.

UNDERSIDE as above, except that the anterior wing has the band white, and a submarginal band of white spots, and that the posterior wing has the base of the costal margin yellow : a short longitudinal band of brick-red from the inner margin, and the band of the outer margin white.

Exp. 3½ inches.

This species was previously in the collection of Mr. Saunders, and belongs to the group of which *H. Cydno* and *Sappho* form part.

15. Heliconia unimaculata.

UPPERSIDE. *Male.*—Dark brown. Anterior wing with a quadrate quinquefid yellow spot beyond the middle, bordered outwardly with carmine.

UNDERSIDE as above, except that the anterior wing has the base carmine, and the spot without its carmine border, that the posterior wing has the costal margin yellow at the base and two carmine spots near it.

Exp. 3 inches.

Unlike any other species : may be a variety of *H. notabilis.*

16. Heliconia Hierax.

UPPERSIDE black. Anterior wing with a band of scarlet (divided by the submedian nervure) from the base outwards : crossed at the middle (at a right angle with the costal margin) by an irregular band of yellow (as in *H. Clysonyma*), commencing on the costal margin by a separate spot, and divided by black nervures into six parts : a small subapical trifid spot of yellow. Posterior wing crossed near the base by a broad band of scarlet, divided into seven parts by black nervures.

UNDERSIDE pale brown. Anterior wing with the band and spot as above. Posterior wing with the base of the costal margin yellow : two scarlet spots near the base : indistinct rays of white on both sides of the nervures from the middle to a series of submarginal white spots.

Exp. 3 inches.

Near to *Clysonyma*; nearer to *Himera*, Hewitson.

Of *Melinæa* and *Mechanitis* one of each is described.

17. Melinæa Mæonis.

UPPERSIDE. *Male.*—Black. Anterior wing with a narrow band from the base following the median nervure and its first branch to near the outer margin where there is a round spot, an oblique band at the middle of the cell, and two spots below this all rufous : a narrow, irregular, oblique band beyond the middle, and three large spots near the apex yellow. Posterior wing rufous, with a band before the middle, a spot near the apex, and the outer margin dark brown.

UNDERSIDE as above, except that the posterior wing has the base yellow, and a broad band of brown near and parallel to the costal margin.

Exp. $3\frac{3}{10}$ inches.

Near to *M. Mælus* of Hewitson.

18. Mechanitis Mantineus.

UPPERSIDE. *Male.*—Black. Anterior wing with a linear spot from the base, an oblong spot within the cell, a small spot below this, and an irregular oblique band beyond the middle pale semitransparent yellow : an orange spot near the anal angle. Posterior wing crossed before the middle by a straight band of pale yellow : beyond the middle by a broken band of orange spots, and by a submarginal series of white spots.

UNDERSIDE as above, except that the anterior wing has a submarginal series of white spots, and that the posterior wing has the base yellow.

Exp. $2\frac{13}{20}$ inches.

Near *M. Menapis* of Hewitson.

One of the gems of the collection is a new species of *Athesis,* larger than *Olyras Crathis.*

19. Athesis Acrisione.

UPPERSIDE. *Male.*—Transparent rufous-white. Anterior wing with the costal margin to the middle, the inner margin which is broad, the outer margin which is narrow, a band at the middle of the cell, a band at the end of the cell, the three branches of the median nervure, and the median nervure between them all black : the apex and the costal and outer margins to their middle rufous-orange : two or three indistinct subapical black spots. Posterior wing with a broad band at the middle, the outer margin, which is broad, and the nervures between them black : a submarginal series of twelve white spots.

UNDERSIDE as above, except that the anterior wing has some small white spots at the apex and on the outer margin towards the anal angle, and that the costal margin of the posterior wing is yellow from the base to the middle, and rufous beyond.

Female does not differ from the male.

Exp. $3\frac{7}{10}$ inches.

One of the most beautiful of the *Heliconidæ.*

Of *Ithomia*, of which there are 70 species, a complete list is given, as in *Leptalis*, to show its great extent. Besides the 20 new species described below, there are several which were previously unique in the British Museum.

Ithomia Mamercus, *n. sp.* I. Mansuetus. I. Achæa, *n. sp.* I. Æmilia, *n. sp.* I. Fluonia. I. Æthra, *n. sp.* I. Antonia, *n. sp.* I. Cornelia. I. Azara. I. Varina, *n. sp.* I. Phagesia, *n. sp.* I. Dero. I. Epidero. I. Alexirrhoë. I. Kezia. I. Virginiana. I Duessa. I. Norella. I. Oulita. I. Iphianassa (*two varieties*). I. Latilla. I. Duillia. I. Alphesibœa, *n. sp.* I. Æginata, *n. sp.* I. Thabena, *n. sp.* I. Zerlina. I. Zavaleta. I. Zabina. I. Epona, *n. sp.* I. Adina. I. Tacuna. I. Cleonica. I. Esula. I. Panthyale. I. Dercetis. I. Andromica. I. Sylvella. I. Apuleia. I. Ticida, *n. sp.* I. Ticidella, *n. sp.* I. Artena. I. Cymothoë. I. Terra. I. Vestella. I. Lilla. I. Salonina. I. Timna. I. Harbona, *n. sp.* I. Makrena. I. Tabera, *n. sp.* I. Cœno. I. Adelinda. I. Cœnina, *n. sp.* I. Antea, *n. sp.* I. Padilla. I. Estella. I. Inachia (*var.* Pharo). I. Agarista. I. Ilerdina. I. Eurimedia. I. Ethica. I. Derasa. I. Lanica, *n. sp.* I. Zelica. I. Zibia. I. Orolina. I. Corena. I. Cydonia. I. Mirza, *n. sp.* I. Alissa, *n. sp.*

20. Ithomia Mamercus.

Mechanitis Mamercus ♀, *Hew. Ent. Monthly Mag.* p. 97, 1869.

Upperside. *Male.*—Orange. Anterior wing crossed beyond the middle by a broad irregular band of yellow, dentated on both sides: the base of the costal margin, a band parallel to the base of the inner margin, a triangular spot between them, three spots (one minute) near the middle, and the apex which is broad, all black. Posterior wing with the neuration of *I. Ninonia* : a large spot which covers nearly half of the wing and is bounded by the inner margin black.

Exp. $2\frac{4}{10}$ inches.

My first description was made from a female. The likeness this species bears to *M. Mansuetus* (which is an *Ithomia*), as well as to *M. Mnemophilus*, is so great, that no one igno-

rant of the perplexing manner in which these genera resemble each other would believe them to be even distinct
species.

21. Ithomia Achæa.

UPPERSIDE. *Male.*—Orange. Antennæ yellow, with the
base brown. Anterior wing with a band from the base, the
base of the costal and inner margins, the apex (broadly), and
two spots at the end of the cell dark brown : a short band
from the costal margin beyond its middle and a small spot
near the anal angle yellow. Posterior wing with the neuration of *Cyrianassa* : dark brown, with a large spot of orange
at the apex.

UNDERSIDE as above, except that there is a submarginal
band of white spots on both wings, that the small yellow spot
near the anal angle of the anterior wing is much larger and
marked by a minute black spot, and that the base of the
posterior wing is yellow.

Exp. 2 inches.

This cannot be compared to any other species; it bears
some resemblance, except in size, to *I. Mansuetus.*

22. Ithomia Antonia.

UPPERSIDE. *Male.*—Orange. Both wings with the
outer margin broadly dark brown, traversed by a series of
large yellow spots. Anterior wing with the costal and
inner margins, a triangular spot in the cell, and a triangular
spot below this black : a broad, short, irregular band of
yellow from the costal margin beyond the middle bordered
on its inner margin and below with black. Posterior wing
with the neuration of *I. Thea* : a longitudinal band of black
spots at the middle.

UNDERSIDE as above, except that there is a band of
brown near the costal margin of the posterior wing.

Exp. $2\frac{4}{10}$ inches.

A very beautiful species, most nearly allied to *I. Thea.*

23. Ithomia Æmilia.

UPPERSIDE. *Male.*—Orange. Anterior wing with the base of the costal and inner margins, three spots in the cell, and the apex (which is broad) dark brown : a broad oblique sinuated band beyond the middle, and five subapical (two of them minute) pale yellow. Posterior wing with the neuration of *I. Ninonia* : a large brown spot at the anal angle.

UNDERSIDE as above, except that the posterior wing has the base of the costal margin yellow, and a band of dark brown near and parallel to the costal margin.

Exp. $2\frac{9}{20}$ inches.

Most like *I. Megalopolis* of Felder.

24. Ithomia Æthra.

UPPERSIDE. *Male.*—Dark brown. Anterior wing with a band from the base (following the median nervure and part of its first branch) and a band near the costal margin orange : a spot in the cell (near the end), an angular band of six spots (the first four touching each other), and a small spot at the apex yellow. Posterior wing with the neuration of *I. Cyrianassa* : orange, with a longitudinal band of four spots, and the outer margin dark brown.

UNDERSIDE as above, except that the anterior wing has a submarginal band of pale yellow spots, and that the posterior has three apical spots of the same colour, that it has a band of brown near the costal margin, and two undefined ochreous spots bordered below with brown near the apex.

Exp. $2\frac{1}{10}$ to $2\frac{1}{2}$ inches.

Unlike any other species; nearest to *I. Fluonia.*

25. Ithomia Varina.

Ithomia Varina, *Hew. Ent. Monthly Mag.* p. 97, 1869.

UPPERSIDE. *Male.*—Semitransparent, rufous : the margins dark brown. Anterior wing unusually long, with the base rufous : a brown spot at the middle of the cell : crossed near the middle by a broad palmate band of pale yellow, marked by two brown spots, and divided into six parts by the nervures : the apical half brown, with the nervures black. Posterior wing with the neuration of *I. Tutia*; the outer margin brown, narrow.

UNDERSIDE as above, except that there are two minute white spots at the apex of each wing.

Exp. $2\frac{8}{10}$ inches.

Colour of *I. Tutia*, shape and size of *I. Jemima*, male.

26. Ithomia Phagesia.

UPPERSIDE. *Male.*—Semitransparent, with several white spots : the margins brown. Anterior wing pale rufous-brown : the base rufous, a large triangular dark brown spot within the cell followed by a white spot also in the cell : two bands, each of five white spots parallel to the outer margin, the first of which commences on the costal margin by a trifid spot : the last spot of each band near the inner margin connected with the other, forming a large lunular spot. Posterior wing rufous, with a large trifid transparent spot near the apex.

UNDERSIDE as above, except that the anterior wing has two apical white spots, and that the posterior wing has the base dark brown, and a submarginal series of white spots.

Exp. $2\frac{7}{10}$ inches.

Somewhat like *I. Jemima*, but more closely allied to *I. Olyras* of Felder. In this species the spur is emitted from the first discocellular nervure of the posterior wing, in *Olyras* from the second.

EQUATORIAL LEPIDOPTERA

COLLECTED BY Mr. BUCKLEY.

DESCRIBED BY
W. C. HEWITSON.

PART II.

LONDON:

JOHN VAN VOORST, 1 PATERNOSTER ROW.

December 15, 1869.

27. Ithomia Alphesibœa.

UPPERSIDE. *Male.*—Transparent. Anterior wing tinted with lilac from the base to the middle, rufous beyond it, with the costal margin (broader from the base to the middle), the inner margin, the nervures, and triangular spots on the outer margin brown : the costal margin from the middle to the apex and spots on the outer margin rufous-orange. Posterior wing lilac-white, the inner margin broadly rufous : the costal margin, a spot at the apex, and a triangular spot at the middle of the outer margin red-brown.

UNDERSIDE as above, except that the costal margin of the posterior wing is broadly rufous, paler at its base.

Exp. $2\frac{7}{10}$ inches.

This species is altogether so much like *I. Duillia* that, but for its great inferiority of size, I should have passed it as the same species. There is, however, considerable difference in the nervures on the costal margin of the posterior wing; and, what is easier to describe and see, on the anterior wing of *I. Duillia* the point or spur is emitted at the end of the cell from the second discocellular nervule, in the new species from the third.

28. Ithomia Ægineta.

UPPERSIDE. *Female.*—Transparent lilac-white, except the apical half of the anterior wing which is tinted with orange. Both wings with the margins broadly black : the outer margins (very broad on the posterior wing) dentated on the inner border : the nervures black, very slender. Anterior wing with a large black spot at the end of the cell, and beyond it a rufous spot on the costal margin. Posterior wing with the neuration of *Zerlina* : a black spot on the costal margin at the end of the cell.

UNDERSIDE as above, except that both wings have a submarginal series of white spots in pairs, except at the

Published December 15, 1869.

apex of both wings and at the anal angle of the posterior
wing, where they are single. Posterior wing with a white
spot at the middle of the costal margin.

Exp. $2\frac{17}{20}$ inches.

This, though unlike any other species, may have a male
not unlike *I. Theudelinda.*

29. Ithomia Thabena.

UPPERSIDE. *Female.*—Transparent : the nervures black.
Anterior wing with a rufous tint : the costal margin (which
is half rufous) and the outer margin (which is dentated inwardly) narrow, the inner margin (which is broad) and a
band at the end of the cell all dark brown : the spot on the
costal margin white. Posterior wing tinted with lilac, with
the neuration of *Zerlina* : the costal margin and the outer
margin (which is very broad) dark brown.

UNDERSIDE as above, except that all the margins and
the band at the end of the cell of the anterior wing are
rufous, that the anterior wing has three minute apical spots
of white, and that the posterior wing has a submarginal
series of white spots in pairs : the apical spot largest and
single.

Exp. $2\frac{7}{10}$ inches.

General appearance of *I. Zerlina.*

30. Ithomia Harbona.

UPPERSIDE. *Male.*—Transparent white : the nervures
black : all the margins of both wings (the abdominal margin
always excepted) broadly dark brown, the outer margins
traversed by a series of obscure pale spots, two of which
at the apex of the anterior wing are most distinct. Anterior
wing with a broad irregular band at the end of the cell : the
usual spot at the costal margin small, white, and bifid.

UNDERSIDE as above, except that the margins and discocellular band are rufous, and that both wings have a submarginal series of distinct white spots.

Exp. $2\frac{9}{10}$ inches.

Form of *I. Makrena*; neuration of *I. Inachia*.

31. Ithomia Tabera.

UPPERSIDE. *Male.*—Transparent lilac-white: the nervures black. Both wings with some apical white spots. Anterior wing with a broad oblique band in the cell, a narrow angular band at the end of the cell dark brown: the discoidal nervures curved and broad near the outer margin: the usual spot on the costal margin, and a second spot near the apex white. Posterior wing with the outer margin very broad.

UNDERSIDE as above, except that the margins and band of the anterior wing are all rufous, and that those of the posterior wing are traversed by a band of the same colour, and that both wings have a submarginal series of distinct white spots.

Exp. $2\frac{6}{10}$ inches.

Form and appearance of *I. Makrena* of which it is probably only a variety.

32. Ithomia Epona.

UPPERSIDE. *Male.*—Transparent rufous-white: the nervures black. Anterior wing with the costal margin and apex rufous: the inner margin broadly dark brown rufous at the median nervure: a triangular spot in the cell, a curved narrow band at the end of the cell, and spots where the nervures meet the outer margin all black. Posterior wing with the neuration of *Zerlina*: the outer margin spotted with brown.

UNDERSIDE as above, except that the marginal spots are rufous, that the base of the posterior wing is pale yellow bordered below with brown, and marked by the singular oval spot which indicates the sex.

Exp. 2½ inches.

The triangular black spot within the cell distinguishes this from all other species.

33. Ithomia Antea.

UPPERSIDE. *Male.*—Transparent white, slightly tinted with lilac: the margins of both wings broadly black: the nervures black. Anterior wing unusually long and pointed, with four subapical white spots.

UNDERSIDE as above, except that the base of the posterior wing is bright yellow, and that both wings have a submarginal series of white spots.

Exp. $2\frac{3}{10}$ to 3 inches.

This species has a close resemblance to a large variety of *I. Cœno*: the neuration is the same. It is always without the yellow tint on the upperside of that species and differs from it also in having the point of the antennæ yellow and the base of the posterior wing on the underside bright yellow.

34. Ithomia Cœnina.

UPPERSIDE. *Male.*—Transparent white, very glossy. Both wings with the margins dark brown: the nervures, which are very slender, black.

UNDERSIDE as above, except that the anterior wing has three subapical white spots, and that the posterior wing has a submarginal series of large white spots.

Exp. $1\frac{17}{20}$ inch.

In colouring like *I. Cœno*; in size the smallest of the group: in the neuration of the posterior wing different from them all, and like *I. Flora*.

35. Ithomia Ticida.

UPPERSIDE. *Male.*—Transparent rufous-white: the base of both wings tinted with orange: the nervures black, slender: the margins dark brown. Anterior wing with the usual costal spot obscure white.

UNDERSIDE as above, except that the costal margin near the apex of the anterior wing is rufous, that there are three subapical snow-white spots, and that the posterior wing has the base yellow, and a submarginal series of five white spots.

Exp. $2\frac{1}{20}$ inches.

Form and neuration of *I. Sylvella.*

36. Ithomia Ticidella.

UPPERSIDE. *Male.*—Transparent white: the margins brown, narrow. Anterior wing with the inner border of the costal and inner margins rufous to the middle of the wing: the costal spot white. Posterior wing rufous near the inner margin.

UNDERSIDE as above, except that the margins are rufous-yellow, that the anterior wing has three apical white spots, and that the posterior wing has its base yellow, and a series of submarginal white spots in pairs.

Exp. $2\frac{3}{20}$ inches.

Neuration and appearance of *I. Sylvella,* but without the black band at the end of the cell. Very nearly allied to the last, but differs from it in having the spur emitted from the lower instead of the middle discocellular nervule of the anterior wing.

37. Ithomia Lamia.

UPPERSIDE. *Male.*—Transparent white, slightly tinted with yellow near the base. Both wings with the outer margin broadly brown traversed by a series of large white spots. Anterior wing with the costal and inner margins brown: crossed at the end of the cell by a band of brown which follows the second branch of the median nervure to the outer margin. Posterior wing with a similar but angular band of brown at the end of the cell, but following the third branch of the median nervure.

UNDERSIDE as above, except that the costal margin of the posterior wing is yellow from its base to its middle.

Exp. $1\frac{17}{20}$ inch.

Much like *I. Ethica* of Hewitson, but with the neuration of *Inachia*.

38. Ithomia Mirza.

I. Lavinia, *Hewitson, Exot. Butt.* vol. i. pl. 15. fig. 34.

39. Ithomia Alissa.

UPPERSIDE. *Female.*—Transparent white : the nervures black. Anterior wing with the costal margin (which is narrow), a triangular curved spot at the end of the cell, the apex (which is broad), and the outer and inner margins all black. A small white spot on the costal margin at the end of the cell. Posterior wing with the costal and outer margins black.

UNDERSIDE as above, except that the margins and band of the anterior wing are all rufous, and that each wing has two apical white spots.

Exp. $1\frac{7}{10}$ inch.

Neuration and size of *I. Vestilla*.

With the resemblance which the genus *Eueides* bears to *Heliconia*, it possesses as well all its liability to vary. Of the species in this collection no two specimens are alike, and in a series of eight of the new species all are different.

40. Eueides Acacetes.

UPPERSIDE. *Male.*—Rufous-orange. Anterior wing

with the base of the costal and inner margins, a band from the base in the cell, a spot at the end of the cell, the apex (which is very broad), and the outer margin dark brown. Posterior wing with the base, a band of five spots in the middle, and the outer margin (which is broad and dentated on its inner border) dark brown.

UNDERSIDE as above, except that the colours are much less bright, that the anterior wing has four subapical white spots, and that the posterior wing has a yellow spot at the base, and a submarginal series of white spots in pairs, except near the apex, where they are single.

Exp. $2\frac{13}{20}$ inches.

ACRÆIDÆ.

41. Acræa albofasciata.

UPPERSIDE dark brown, paler towards the base of both wings. Anterior wing crossed beyond the middle by a transverse band of white divided by the nervures into six parts.

UNDERSIDE pale brown. Anterior wing with the base slightly rufous : the band broader than above with its inner border dark brown : the apex beyond it with the nervures and lines between them black. Posterior wing darker brown near the outer margin, the nervures and lines between them black.

Exp. $2\frac{1}{2}$ inches.

Nearest to *A. Hylonome,* but much larger and with the band nearer the apex.

NYMPHALIDÆ.

In this family *Eresia* produces the greatest number of species. There are 25, ten of which are new. There is a

very beautiful series of *E. Pelonia,* the ordinary female of
which is *E. Ithomiola* of Salvin ; another female, which I had
described as a new species and was very unwilling to relin-
quish, has the apical half of the anterior wing marked by
seven large yellow spots, several of which are indicated in
one of the males. There is also a remarkable species nearly
related to *E. Phædima* of Salvin, and one, which is described under the name of *Elæa,* differs in form from any
known species.

42. Eresia Ildica.

UPPERSIDE. *Female.*—Both wings with a submarginal
series of white spots. Anterior wing yellow-grey irrorated
throughout with brown, rufous towards the inner margin :
the nervures and the costal and outer margins dark brown,
broad. Posterior wing orange, with the costal and outer
margins dark brown, broad.

UNDERSIDE as above, except that the anterior wing has
the base pale yellow.

Exp. $2\frac{7}{10}$ inches.

Nearest to *E. Phædima* of Salvin.

43. Eresia Letitia.

UPPERSIDE. *Female.*—Dark brown, crossed by a broad
tripartite band, which, after nearly filling the cell, curves
towards the outer margin where it is followed by a bifid
spot : a triangular spot (which is divided into four by the
nervures) beyond the middle of the costal margin, a large trifid
spot between this and the apex, and a submarginal series
of spots all pale rufous. Posterior wing crossed longitudinally before the middle by a broad pale rufous band intersected by black nervures : a submarginal band of lunular
spots, and an apical white spot.

UNDERSIDE as above, except that both wings have a
submarginal black line, and that there is a double series of

lunular pale spots near the outer margin of the posterior wing.

Exp. $2\frac{1}{10}$ inches.

I cannot compare this to any other species. There is a female variety in which the bands and spots are all white.

44. Eresia Casiphia.

UPPERSIDE. *Male.*—Dark brown. Anterior wing with a band from the base, a trifid irregular oblique band at the middle, and a subapical band of four spots (the first minute) all rufous-orange. Posterior wing crossed longitudinally before the middle by a broad band of rufous-orange intersected by black nervures and by a submarginal band of the same colour: a minute spot of white at the apex.

UNDERSIDE as above, except that the bands and spots are paler, that both wings have a submarginal series of white spots, that the anterior wing has three apical white spots besides, and that the submarginal band of the posterior wing is broader.

Exp. 2 inches.

Most like *E. Eranites* in form and colour.

45. Eresia Elæa.

UPPERSIDE. *Female.*—Dark brown. Anterior wing with an oblique band of scarlet at the middle divided into four spots by the nervures: the first spot, which is nearer the base than the others, is within the cell and quadrate.

UNDERSIDE. Anterior wing as above, except that the apex is broadly pale brown, with the nervures and lines between them black, and that the three lower spots of the band are extended to the outer margin and there intersected by black lines between the nervures. Posterior wing pale brown, with the nervures, lines between them, and a submarginal line black : two spots near the base and part of the outer margin scarlet.

Exp. $1\frac{17}{20}$ inch.

Nearest to *E. Castilla* of Felder.

46. Eresia Sestia.

UPPERSIDE.   *Male.*—Dark brown.   Anterior wing crossed from the base, curving towards the outer margin (having the median nervure and its first branch for its lower border), by a band of rufous-orange divided into three parts by the nervures, and into a fourth part at its lower extremity (where there is a minute spot) by a black line : crossed before the apex by a band of seven spots, the first on the costal margin minute, the others in pairs.   Posterior wing crossed longitudinally before the middle by a broad band of rufous-orange intersected by black nervures : a subapical yellow spot and a submarginal band of linear white spots.

UNDERSIDE as above, except that the spots of the anterior wing are yellow and much larger, and that there is a submarginal band of spots of the same colour, that the posterior wing has the central band broader and paler, that the base, a band near it, and a submarginal band of spots are all pale yellow : four small white spots near the anal angle.

Female like the male, except that all the spots and bands on both sides are pale yellow or white.

Exp. ♂ $1\frac{8}{10}$, ♀ 2 inches.

Nearest to *E. Eranites* of Hewitson.

47. Eresia Mylitta.

UPPERSIDE.   *Male.*—Dark brown.   Anterior wing with a broad band from the base (which runs parallel with the inner margin, and occupies one-third of the wing) and a large subapical spot divided into four parts by the nervures rufous-orange.   Posterior wing with a broad central band (occupying more than half the wing) and a narrow band from the anal angle to the middle rufous-orange.

UNDERSIDE as above, except that the subapical spot is yellow, that there are some white spots in a double series at the apex, that the posterior wing has the base and a band near it yellow, the central band paler, and a submarginal linear band of white.

Exp. $1\frac{8}{10}$ inch.

Much like a small example of *Eueides Aliphera*.

48. Eresia Neria.

E. Neria, *Hewitson, Entom. Monthly Mag.* p. 98, Oct. 1869.

UPPERSIDE. *Male.*—Dark brown. Anterior wing with a large triangular basal spot of rufous-orange divided by the nervures : the nervure which closes the cell broad and black.

UNDERSIDE rufous-brown, with the nervures and lines between them black. Anterior wing with the basal spot as above. Posterior wing irrorated with yellow : the base yellow, with two red spots near it.

Exp. $1\frac{8}{10}$ inch.

Nearest to *E. Acræina* and *Perilla*.

49. Eresia Tissa.

UPPERSIDE. *Male.*—Uniform dark brown : the fringe narrow, white.

UNDERSIDE rufous undulated with darker colour. Anterior wing broadly orange-yellow below the median nervure from the base to beyond the middle : crossed beyond the middle by a rufous-brown band.

Exp. $1\frac{3}{20}$ inch.

Shape and size of *E. Anieta*, which it also resembles on the underside.

50. Eresia trimaculata.

UPPERSIDE. *Male.*—Dark brown. The base of both wings thickly irrorated with rufous-yellow. Anterior wing crossed beyond the middle by three spots of orange,—the first spot near the costal margin large and oblong, the second and third round at an angle with the first : between these spots and the outer margin there are two linear spots of the same colour, and on the margin two white spots : a subapical white spot. Posterior wing crossed below the middle by three linear bands of lunules : those of the first two bands placed *vis-à-vis* : the fringe white.

UNDERSIDE. Anterior wing rufous-brown : the base broadly yellow crossed by two brown lines : the three spots of the upperside united : the apex and a spot on the outer margin ochreous-yellow : a submarginal series of lunular white spots. Posterior wing rufous : the base yellow marked by several white spots : an irregular band of white spots at the middle : a rufous spot on the costal margin : a band of dark brown spots beyond the middle, and a submarginal band of white lunular spots : the apex yellow.

Exp. $1\frac{4}{10}$ inch.

Size and form of *E. Acesas.*

51. Eresia Alceta.

UPPERSIDE. *Female.*—Dark rufous-brown. Both wings with rufous undulations near the base. Anterior wing with two small spots within the cell, two near the inner margin, a transverse broken band beyond the middle followed by a spot near the apex, two round spots below this wide apart, and three submarginal lunular spots all rufous-orange. Posterior wing crossed by a central band followed by two bands of lunular spots all orange.

UNDERSIDE. Anterior wing dark brown, with the band and spots as above : a band at the base and two spots within the cell orange-yellow bordered with black : a submarginal band of rufous lunular spots: the margin rufous: the apex spotted with lilac. Posterior wing variegated from the base to the middle with grey and brown bordered outwardly with dark brown followed by a rufous band, by a band of white, by a band of dark brown spots, and by a submarginal band of lunular spots bordered below with brown.

Exp. $1\frac{9}{10}$ inch.

Size and form of *E. Acesas.*

Although there is no new species to record in the genus *Catagramma,* there is a fine series of several species which have until now been very rare—*C. Excelsior, C. Hesperis,* and *C. Maimuna* of the two varieties which occur in *C. Eunomia,* carmine in one, orange-yellow in the other.

When I figured *C. Alicia* as a species distinct from *C. Vaninka,* it was with considerable hesitation. I have now, however, a series of each, and find that, besides the differences then pointed out in the form of the transverse band of the anterior wing and the presence of an apical spot of blue, the bands on the underside of the posterior wing of *Alicia* are much nearer together.

In *Callithea* Mr. Buckley had the good fortune to take a new and very distinct species, as well as several specimens of the rare *C. Degandii,* and a fine series of *C. Markii.*

52. Callithea Buckleyi.

UPPERSIDE. *Male.*—Very dark violet-blue with the outer margins green.

UNDERSIDE glossy green. Anterior wing with the base orange broadly bordered outwardly by blue-black: three small subapical black spots. Posterior wing with the basal half orange narrowly bordered with black and followed by a transverse band of nine very black round spots and two linear bands of blue-black.

Exp. $2\frac{6}{10}$ inches.

Easily known from all the other species by having only one submarginal row of spots on the underside of the posterior wing.

In *Agrias,* as in *Callithea,* there is a glorious new species closely resembling *A. Phalcidon* on the upperside, and as much like *A. Hewitsonius* on the underside. There are perfect specimens of the rare *A. Sardanapalus.*

53. Agrias Beatifica.

UPPERSIDE. *Male.*—Brilliant dark blue. Both wings with a broad marginal band of grey-green. Anterior wing with the costal margin, the apex, and an indistinct band near it black: the nervures black. Posterior wing with the base, the costal and inner margins black.

UNDERSIDE. Anterior wing grey-blue: the basal half (except the base which is scarlet) blue-black: a small black spot at each side of the discocellular nervure, and beyond it two small black spots. Posterior wing grey-green, with the base and inner margin to beyond the end of the cell scarlet: a minute spot within the cell, and a second on the discocellular nervure brown: crossed by four bands of black spots,—the first band short, of four spots: the second of seven: the third of seven which are round or oval each marked by one minute spot of white except that which is nearest the anal angle which has two: the fourth band submarginal, of seven linear spots.

Exp. 3½ inches.

In the genus *Prepona* there are specimens of *P. Licomedes* of Cramer, a butterfly for which I have been long on the watch.

There is a large and splendid series of *Pandora Hypochlora* of both sexes of that variety, with the underside of the posterior wing yellow, which Mr. Salvin has described under the name of *Hemichrysa*. I would gladly adopt the generic name which Dr. Felder has given to this species were it not at the expense of scientific accuracy, since it scarcely differs at all from *Pandora*.

Siderone Archidona is another of the choice things of this collection.

---

54. Paphia Vestina.

UPPERSIDE. *Male.*—Anterior wing blue-black with the base broadly grassy green : crossed by a submarginal band of six green spots, the first spot near the costal margin at a distance from the apex : the outer margin brown : the inner margin sinuate. Posterior wing rufous-brown, with a broad curved longitudinal band of green.

UNDERSIDE glossy red-brown irrorated with paler colour. Anterior wing crossed from the apex to the middle of the inner margin by a band of dark brown bordered outwardly with white : the outer margin white. Posterior wing crossed by a band of brown bordered outwardly with white from the costal margin before the middle to the middle of the wing : crossed beyond the middle by two dark brown bands from the apex to the inner margin near the anal angle partly bordered with white. Both wings with some indistinct submarginal white spots.

Exp. $2\frac{7}{10}$ inches.

The bands of the underside arranged as in *P. Philumena*.

MORPHIDÆ.

In *Morpho* Mr. Buckley took a single example of *M. Eugenia*, and a very beautiful thing, which I must either describe as new, or consider it, together with *M. Egyptus*, as

a variety of *Hecuba*. It is as large as either of these : has
the upperside of *Telemachus* of Cramer, and on its underside
the oblong ocelli as on the posterior wing of *Egyptus*.

55. Morpho Phanodemus.

UPPERSIDE. *Male.*—Dark brown. Both wings crossed
from the costal margin beyond the middle of the anterior
wing to the inner margin of the posterior wing by a broad
band of silvery grey, narrow at its commencement on the
anterior wing where it is tinted with rufous-orange, and very
broad at the inner margin of the posterior wing. Outer
margin of the anterior wing with lunular white spots : of the
posterior wing with white spots in pairs. Posterior wing
with a submarginal series of rufous spots.

UNDERSIDE as in *M. Egyptus* (*Cisseis* of Felder, Wien.
ent. Monats. pl. 4 : 1860).

56. Narope Nesope.

UPPERSIDE. *Male.*—Dark rufous-brown. Anterior
wing from the costal margin to the median nervures (except
towards the apex) and the outer margin rufous-orange : a
black line at the end of the cell, and below this a large round
dark brown silk-like spot. Posterior wing with the outer
margin rufous.

UNDERSIDE rufous, undulated with darker colour. Anterior wing with the base, a broad band near it, a second
band beyond the middle (broad near the costal margin and
marked by a white spot) all brown : the apex lilac : three
minute submarginal black spots. Posterior wing brown,
marked near the base by a spot of darker brown, and lower
down by three pale rufous spots : crossed from the costal
margin to the anal angle by a band of brown bordered outwardly with white below the middle, and marked by a series
of minute black spots, two of which, nearest the anal angle,
are centred with white.

Exp. $2\frac{2}{10}$ inches.

EQUATORIAL LEPIDOPTERA

COLLECTED BY Mr. BUCKLEY.

DESCRIBED BY
W. C. HEWITSON.

PART III.

LONDON:

JOHN VAN VOORST, 1 PATERNOSTER ROW.

December 30, 1869.

SATYRIDÆ.

The only species of much interest in this family, besides the new ones, are the remarkable *Antirrhæa Geryon* of Felder, and the *Lymanopoda Acræida* of Butler.

57. Pronophila Tena.

P. Tena, *Hewitson, Ent. Monthly Mag.* p. 98, Oct. 1869.

UPPERSIDE. *Female.*—Dark rufous-brown. Anterior wing crossed beyond the middle by a band of four or five white spots : two minute white spots near the apex. Posterior wing crossed beyond the middle by a series of three or four minute white spots.

UNDERSIDE as above, except that both wings are undulated with paler colour near their outer margins and that the spots of the anterior wing are smaller.

Exp. 2 inches.

Unlike any other species, but nearest to *P. Perita* of Hewitson. The males of this species have the white spots much smaller and in some specimens scarcely visible on either side. This species was taken on the margin of the snow on the Cordilleras.

58. Pronophila Pomponia.

UPPERSIDE. *Male.*—Dark brown. Anterior wing with the outer margin broadly ferruginous. Posterior wing dentated.

UNDERSIDE dark brown undulated throughout with paler colour and irrorated with white on the posterior wing. Anterior wing with two indistinct bands within the cell, and a submarginal broad equal band of pale yellow undulated with brown and bordered on both sides with black. Posterior wing with a submarginal unequal band somewhat paler

D

Published December 30, 1869.

than the rest of the wing, bordered on both sides with black and marked near the apex and anal angle by a single white spot.

Exp. $2\frac{3}{20}$ inches.

Form and size of small examples of *P. Polusca*.

59. Pronophila Porcia.

UPPERSIDE. *Male*.—Dark brown, slightly paler beyond the middle of the anterior wing, the fringe indistinctly spotted with white. Posterior wing dentate, the fringe grey.

UNDERSIDE dark rufous-brown. The anterior wing beyond the middle and the whole of the posterior wing undulated with paler colour. Anterior wing indistinctly marked with white on the costal margin beyond the middle. Posterior wing *crossed* from the costal margin beyond its middle to the third median nervule *by a band of yellow* broken and narrower at its terminus.

Exp. $2\frac{2}{10}$ inches.

Size and form of *P. Prytanis*.

60. Pronophila Alusana.

P. Alusana, *Hew. Ent. Monthly Mag.* p. 98, 1869.

UPPERSIDE. *Male*.—Dark brown, the outer margins dentated. Anterior wing crossed at the middle by a broad irregular band of orange. Posterior wing crossed beyond the middle by a similar band of orange broken near the apex, where a portion of it forms a triangular spot.

UNDERSIDE as above, except that the anterior wing is ochreous near the apex which is crossed by a band of four minute white spots, that the posterior wing is crossed before the middle by an angular broken band of white, that the apical spot (which is much larger and undulated with brown) is united with the band which is also slightly undulated with brown, and that the space between the band and the outer margin is undulated with ochreous-yellow and has three triangular spots of lilac-white, each marked by a white spot bordered with black.

Exp. 2 inches.

Nearly allied to *P. Philotera* of Hewitson.

61. Pronophila Panacea.

UPPERSIDE. *Male.*—Dark brown. Anterior wing paler towards the outer margin.

UNDERSIDE dark rufous-brown. Anterior wing towards the margins and the whole of the posterior wing undulated with darker brown. Anterior wing with two black ocelli (each with a pupil of white) between the median nervules, and between them and the apex a minute white spot. Posterior wing crossed beyond the middle by a series of minute black ocelli, some of which have white pupils.

Female.—Rufous-brown. Anterior wing paler towards the outer margin, and marked by four ocelli with pale rufous border and pupil of white, the two nearest the apex small. Underside as in the male, but much paler.

Exp. $1\frac{15}{20}$ inch.

This species varies much with regard to the ocelli on the underside. One specimen is without any except one of those on the anterior wing.

Nearest to *P. Manis* of Felder in size and form.

62. Euptychia cœlica.

UPPERSIDE. *Male.*—Cerulean blue. Anterior wing with the costal margin beyond the middle, the apex, and outer margin broadly dark brown. Posterior wing with the apex, a line between the third median and discoidal nervures, a submarginal line, and the margin dark brown.

UNDERSIDE cerulean blue. Both wings crossed before the middle by two bands: both with two submarginal bands and the margin dark brown. Anterior wing with a short band of brown from the costal margin beyond its middle, marked by a black ocellus bordered with brown. Posterior wing with three black ocelli: two near the apex (the first small) and one towards the anal angle, and between them two black caudate outline spots of brown.

Exp. 2 inches.

Greatly excels in beauty any of the allied blue species.

63. Euptychia albofasciata.

UPPERSIDE. *Female.*—Rufous-brown. Both wings crossed from the third median nervure of the anterior wing to the inner margin nearly of the posterior wing by a broad central band of white. Posterior wing with one large black ocellus towards the anal angle bordered with orange, the pupil white: two submarginal bands of white indistinct towards the apex.

UNDERSIDE rufous-brown, with the band as above, except that it extends to the costal margin of the anterior wing. Both wings with the base grey, crossed by a band of brown: both with the outer margin broadly dull white, traversed by two bands of brown: the outer margin also brown. Anterior wing with one apical ocellus bordered with orange, the pupil white. Posterior wing with four ocelli: two near the apex (the first small), and two near the anal angle (the last small), all bordered with orange: the two apical and last anal ocelli bipupillated. Between these ocelli two oval spots, bordered with orange, each marked by two white silver striæ.

Exp. 2 inches.

Nearest to *E. Nossis* of Hewitson.

64. Euptychia Ashna.

UPPERSIDE rufous-brown. Posterior wing with a spot near the anal angle and two submarginal lines black.

UNDERSIDE rufous-brown. Both wings crossed near the base by a band of brown : both with two submarginal lines and the outer margin black. Anterior wing crossed beyond the middle by a band of brown. Posterior wing crossed beyond the middle *by a broad band of white,* followed by three black ocelli (one of which near the apex is small), each with a rufous border and silvery-white pupil, that nearest the anal angle with two : two silver spots between these ocelli.

Exp. $1\frac{11}{20}$ inch.

Nearest to *E. pronophila* of Butler.

65. Euptychia Tiessa.

UPPERSIDE. *Male.*—Dark brown with a submarginal black line. Posterior wing dentated, marked by an indistinct ocellus bordered with brick-red near the anal angle.

UNDERSIDE brown from the base to the middle. Both wings crossed before the middle by a band of red-brown, and at the middle by a broader band of the same colour partly within the cells of both, followed by a broad band of grey traversed by a band of brown marked near the costal margin of the anterior wing by one small ocellus, on the posterior wing by three, two near the apex (the first smallest) and one towards the anal angle, all black with rufous iris bordered with dark brown and pupil of white. Both wings with two submarginal bands and the outer margin red-brown : the band of the posterior wing dentated like the margin.

Exp. $2\frac{3}{10}$ inches.

Richly coloured on the underside. Specimens are in my collection from Quito, and also from Chontales, collected by Mr. Belt.

ERYCINIDÆ.

In this family there are several new and brilliant species. In *Mesosemia* there are 31 species, 13 of which have been described as new ; one of them, *M. Loruhama*, surpasses in beauty any of those hitherto made known.   There are several specimens of *M. Phelina* of Felder.

66. Mesosemia Marsidia.

UPPERSIDE.   *Female.*—Rufous-brown, darker near the outer margins.   Both wings crossed by a common band of white broadest on the anterior wing, not reaching the anal angle of the posterior wing.   Anterior wing with a large discal black spot marked by three minute white spots, and bordered outwardly with orange, and again with brown : three subapical white spots.

UNDERSIDE as above, except that the discal spot is surrounded with orange, that there is a band of orange bordered on both sides with brown at the middle of the cell, that there is a submarginal series of six white spots, and two similar spots nearer the margin, that the nervures between these spots are rufous, and that the posterior wing has two or three marginal white spots.

Exp. 2 inches.

Near to *M. Mænades* of Hewitson.   A variety of this species is without the white band of the posterior wing, having a small spot only of white at the apex.

67. Mesosemia Marsena.

UPPERSIDE.   *Female.*—Dark brown.   Anterior wing with the base, which is marked by three black spots, and a broad transverse band beyond the middle (which is divided into eight parts by the nervures) transparent lilac-white : the discal spot black, triangular, bordered by orange and marked by three minute white spots : two submarginal bands of white spots : the first band of eight spots, the outer band of three. Posterior wing transparent lilac-white from the base to beyond the middle : the nervures black.

UNDERSIDE as above, except that both wings have the nervures rufous, and that the posterior wing has a marginal band of white spots.

Exp. 2 inches.

A most elegant species, nearest to *M. Phelina* of Felder.

68. Mesosemia Ama.

UPPERSIDE. *Female.*—Rufous-brown, with the outer margins dark brown. Both wings crossed at the middle by a band of black, and towards the outer margin by a band of white, broadest near the costal margin of the anterior wing, clouded near the anal angle of the posterior wing. Anterior wing with the black discal spot with a rufous border and three minute spots of white : a black spot between it and the base.

UNDERSIDE as above, except that the posterior wing has a small oblong discal spot marked at both ends with white, and between it and the base a short brown band, and that the white band is scarcely seen except near the apex.

Exp. $1\frac{8}{10}$ inch.

69. Mesosemia Adida.

UPPERSIDE. *Female.*—Rufous-brown, the outer margins broadly dark brown. Both wings crossed beyond the middle by a band of white, broadest on the anterior wing. Anterior wing with the black discal spot marked by three distinct white dots, its border rufous : and on each side of it two bands of brown. Posterior wing crossed beyond the middle by two brown bands.

UNDERSIDE as above, except that the posterior wing has a small discal spot marked by two white dots, with two bands of brown between it and the base.

Exp. $1\frac{15}{20}$ inch.

This and the last-described species come nearest to *M. Telegone* in the angular form of the posterior wing.

70. Mesosemia Zorea.

UPPERSIDE. *Male.*—Green-blue, with the outer margins broadly dark brown. Anterior wing with the black discal spot marked by two white dots: a transverse black band on each side of it. Posterior wing with a black line and spot on the costal margin before its middle and a transverse band of black at the middle.

UNDERSIDE grey-brown. Both wings with the discal black spots each marked by two dots of white, the border broadly rufous: both with a short double band towards the base broken on the anterior wing, both crossed beyond the spots by a pale grey band bordered outwardly with brown, both crossed beyond the middle by a broad band of brown bordered on both sides with grey. Anterior wing with a submarginal brown band. Posterior wing with a series of brown spots crowned with paler colour.

Female.—On both sides as on the underside of the male.

Exp. $1\frac{1}{2}$ inch.

Nearest to *M. Meeda* of Hewitson.

71. Mesosemia latifasciata.

UPPERSIDE. *Male.*—Rufous-brown near the base, dark brown near the outer margins. Both wings crossed by a continuous very broad immaculate white band. Anterior wing with a small black almost triangular discal spot bordered with orange.

Underside as above.

Female like the male, except that it is larger and of a paler brown.

Exp. ♂ $1\frac{17}{20}$, ♀ $2\frac{2}{10}$ inches.

72. Mesosemia Ahava.

Upperside. *Male.*—Dark brown. Anterior wing with the black discal spot marked by three white dots: a very slight indication of a pale brown band before the apex. Posterior wing with the outer half white bordered above with grey crossed by two black lines, a black spot at the apex: the outer margin black, the fringe white.

Underside paler brown. Anterior wing with the discal spot as above, but with a rufous border and encircled by two black bands: crossed transversely from margin to margin by a submarginal band of white. Posterior wing with a minute black discal spot bordered on both sides by three bands of black: broadly white towards the outer margin (which is black) and marked by some dark brown spots.

Exp. $1\frac{6}{10}$ inch.

Belongs to the group of which *M. Metope* is one.

73. Mesosemia Zanoa.

Upperside. *Male.*—Dark brown. Anterior wing with the discal black spot marked by two minute white dots. Posterior wing cerulean blue, with the base and costal margin dark brown: the outer margin with a narrow black line.

Underside rufous-brown. Anterior wing with the discal spot marked by three dots of white, and encircled by three bands of black: crossed near the outer margin by a band of white. Posterior wing with a small black discal spot with three transverse bands of dark brown on each side of it: the outer margin broadly pale blue traversed by a broken line of brown.

Exp. $1\frac{9}{20}$ inch.

Nearest to *M. Philocles*.

74. Mesosemia Mehida.

UPPERSIDE. *Male.*—Brilliant blue. Both wings with a submarginal band and the outer margin black.

UNDERSIDE brown. Both wings crossed beyond the middle by a grey band (zigzag on the posterior wing), by a black line bordered on both sides with grey, and by a submarginal band of black spots. Anterior wing with a black discal spot bordered with orange and marked by one minute white dot, and surrounded alternately by bands of brown, grey, and brown. Posterior wing crossed before the middle by a broad band of brown bordered on each side alternately by bands of grey, brown, grey, and brown, and marked by the discal black spot with a rufous border and two dots of white.

Exp. $1\frac{9}{20}$ inch.

Cannot be compared with any other species, but is most like *M. Meeda* of Hewitson.

75. Mesosemia Zikla.

UPPERSIDE. *Female.*—Cerulean blue. Anterior wing with the black discal spot marked by one white dot and encircled on both sides by two bands of black (the outer band broad and angular near the anal angle) followed by a broad white band : the outer margin dark brown. Posterior wing crossed by six black bands : the outer margin brown.

UNDERSIDE as above, except that it is grey instead of blue, that the discal spot of the anterior wing is bordered with orange-yellow and has a black spot below it, and that there are two submarginal black lines.

Exp. $1\frac{4}{10}$ inch.

Might be the female of *M. Ozora,* but is without the discal spot of the posterior wing.

76. Mesosemia Ozora.

UPPERSIDE. *Male.*—Bright blue. Anterior wing with the black discal spot marked by one minute spot, followed by a short line, by a curved band of black, and by a band of white, beyond which the wing is dark brown. Posterior wing with a spot on the costal margin, four transverse bands, and the outer margin dark brown.

UNDERSIDE pale grey and brown. Both wings with a discal black spot with rufous border and marked by two minute white spots. Anterior wing crossed on each side of the spot by three bands of brown : the white band as above bordered outwardly with dark brown : a submarginal black line. Posterior wing crossed between the spot and the base by four bands of brown : beyond it by six, the fifth broader than the rest.

Exp. $1\frac{3}{10}$ inch.

In colour most like *M. Mevania;* in size and shape very different.

77. Mesosemia Loruhama.

UPPERSIDE. *Male.*—Brilliant blue, tinted with green : the margins brown. Anterior wing with a large black discal spot marked by three minute white spots, a black spot below it, and on each side of them a transverse black linear band : the line between them and the base broken where it crosses the median nervure : crossed beyond the middle by a narrow straight short band of white : the apex broadly dark brown. Posterior wing with a black linear spot at the middle of the costal margin.

UNDERSIDE dark brown. Anterior wing with the spots and lines as above, except that the spots are bordered with orange, and the lines inwardly with paler brown. Posterior wing with a discal spot marked by two minute white spots, a dark brown transverse band bordered inwardly with paler brown on each side of it: a submarginal band of dark brown spots bordered above with white.

Exp. $1\frac{15}{20}$ inch.

Near to *M. Mevania*, nearer to *M. Macrina* of Felder, but does not agree with his description. In some specimens the white band is nearly absent, in others it is broad, and reaches to the anal angle.

78. Mesosemia Reba.

UPPERSIDE. *Male.*—Dark blue tinted with green. Both wings crossed near the base by a band (broken on the anterior wing), both crossed beyond the middle by a second band, and also by a submarginal band all black: the outer margin brown. Anterior wing with a black discal spot marked by two minute white spots: crossed at the second band by a short band of white.

UNDERSIDE rufous-brown. Both wings crossed before the middle by an undulated band of brown: its outer border rufous: both crossed beyond the middle by a similar band (angular on the anterior wing), its inner border rufous: both crossed by a submarginal band of brown spots bordered inwardly with paler colour. Anterior wing with the discal spot bordered with rufous-orange: the white band broader and longer bordered outwardly with dark brown. Posterior wing with a small black discal spot marked by one minute white spot, crossed near the outer margin by some indistinct white spots.

Exp. $1\frac{4}{10}$ inch.

Near to *M. Meletia* of Felder; near, also, to *M. Zorea* described above.

79. Eurybia Jemima.

UPPERSIDE. *Male.*—Dark rufous-brown. Both wings with a submarginal series of large blue-black spots broadly bordered with orange : the apical spot of both wings imperfect. Anterior wing with a black discal spot bordered with orange : two minute spots beyond the discal spot, and beyond these a transverse series of five similar spots rufous : two minute white spots near the costal margin. Posterior wing with two minute rufous spots between the median nervules.

UNDERSIDE as above, except that it is paler brown, and that the submarginal spots are much less conspicuous, that the posterior wing has a small discal black spot bordered above and below with orange, and that there are several minute rufous spots beyond the middle.

Exp. $2\frac{1}{10}$ inches.

80. Cremna Calitra.

UPPERSIDE. *Male.*—Dark brown. Both wings with the basal half marked by several blue spots : both crossed beyond the middle by two bands of hastate blue spots, the first commencing at the costal margin of the anterior wing by a large quadrifid white spot, the second band by three minute white spots : both with a submarginal band of white spots.

UNDERSIDE as above, except that all the spots are white.

Exp. $1\frac{6}{10}$ inch.

Near to *C. Ceneus.*

Of. *Eurygona* there are 29 species, 6 of which are new. Amongst them a fine series of the beautiful *E. Erythræa* described by Mr. Bates from his own collection.

81. Eurygona Athena.

UPPERSIDE. *Female.*—Dark rufous-brown : the outer half of the posterior wing (which is rounded at the outer margin) orange.

UNDERSIDE rufous-grey. Both wings crossed at the middle by a rufous-orange band, paler on the posterior wing and bordered on both sides with brown : both crossed beyond the middle by a less-defined rufous band which ceases at the middle of the posterior wing. Anterior wing darker towards the outer margin. Posterior wing with its outer half orange-yellow : the outer margin orange : a submarginal band of eight white spots, with a rufous border on both sides, except the middle spot (which is crowned by a black spot) and the three spots nearest the anal angle (which are bordered above and below with black).

Exp. $1\frac{6}{10}$ inch.

82. Eurygona Bettinà.

UPPERSIDE. *Male.*—Dark brown, paler towards the apex of the anterior wing.

UNDERSIDE glossy golden white. Posterior wing with a single minute black spot at the middle of the outer margin.

Exp. $1\frac{3}{10}$ inch.

Altogether like *E. Eusepus* of Hewitson, except that it is without the band of the underside, which has a golden tint instead of the silvery white of *Eusepus.*

83. Eurygona Effima.

UPPERSIDE. *Male.*—Dark brown, with the anal angle of the posterior wing broadly white.

UNDERSIDE pale brown : the outer margins brown. Both wings crossed by three bands of brown. Anterior wing with a submarginal band of brown marked at its middle by a black spot. Posterior wing with a submarginal series of black spots bordered below with white : the third spot from the apex larger than the rest.

Exp. $1\frac{2}{10}$ inch.

Does not differ from *E. Euryone,* except in the white at the anal angle. On the upperside it has the appearance of a small specimen of *E. Phedica.*

84. Eurygona onorata.

UPPERSIDE. *Male.*—Rufous. Anterior wing with the centre orange : the costal margin and a quadrate spot at the end of the cell (which is darker but forms part of it), the apex, and outer margin dark brown. Posterior wing with the outer margin from the apex to the middle brown.

UNDERSIDE. Anterior wing grey-brown, with three central white spots. Posterior wing white, with the base, a band from the costal margin to the middle, a curved line below this, and the apex brown : a black spot bordered with white near the middle of the outer margin.

Exp. $1\frac{3}{10}$ inch.

In form like *E. Midas.*

85. Eurygona Issoria.

UPPERSIDE. *Male.*—Uniform dark brown, tinted with purple near the outer margins. Posterior wing much produced, pointed at the anal angle.

UNDERSIDE pale grey-brown. Both wings crossed beyond the middle by a rufous straight band, followed on both by an ill-defined band of brown : the fringe rufous. Posterior wing with a black spot near the middle of the outer margin bordered by paler colour, and between it and the apex some scarcely visible smaller spots.

Exp. 1½ inch.

Form nearly and size of *E. Euodias*.

86. Eurygona præclara.

UPPERSIDE. *Male.*—Orange. Anterior wing with the costal margin and apex (which is broad) dark brown. Posterior wing with the apex brown.

UNDERSIDE. Both wings crossed beyond the middle by a series of pale grey spots, and by a submarginal series of minute brown spots. Anterior wing crossed at the middle by a band of four rufous spots. Posterior wing with a spot near the base, three spots at the middle, and three spots near the anal angle all rufous.

Exp. 1$\frac{7}{10}$ inch.

Very near to *E. opalina*, from which it differs in having the apex more pointed and broadly bordered with brown. I have described it as seen with its head from the light. When reversed it is one of the most glorious things in this part of the Creation, surpassing the *Morphos*.

87. Necyria Juturna.

UPPERSIDE. *Female.*—Dark brown. Anterior wing crossed by a band of carmine from the middle of the costal margin to the outer margin beyond its middle where it curves and runs parallel to the outer margin to the anal angle.

UNDERSIDE as above, except that the wings are blue-brown, with the nervures broad and black, and that the band of the anterior wing is paler and broader.

Exp. 2 inches.

Very nearly allied to *N. Hewitsonii* of Saunders, but without the blue submarginal band on the posterior wing of that species.

EQUATORIAL LEPIDOPTERA

COLLECTED BY Mr. BUCKLEY.

DESCRIBED BY
W. C. HEWITSON.

PART IV.

LONDON:

JOHN VAN VOORST, 1 PATERNOSTER ROW.

March 10, 1870.

88. Erycina pulchra.

UPPERSIDE. *Male.*—Black. Anterior wing crossed before the middle by a broad band of carmine. Posterior wing crossed obliquely by a narrow band of brilliant blue, and by a series of white spots, two of which, nearest the anal angle, are bordered by blue: the outer margin spotted with white.

UNDERSIDE black, with the base of both wings and a band which crosses each of them brilliant blue : a spot of carmine on the inner margin and some spots below this (part of the band of blue) white.

Exp. $1\frac{7}{10}$ inch.

89. Erycina formosa.

UPPERSIDE. *Male.*—Black. Anterior wing crossed before the middle from the costal margin to the anal angle by a slightly curved band of carmine. Posterior wing crossed obliquely from the costal margin beyond the middle to the anal angle (where it is so broad as to fill up nearly the whole of that projecting portion of the wing common to this genus) by a band of white : the outer margin spotted with white.

UNDERSIDE black, with the base and a broad band which crosses both wings brilliant blue. Anterior wing with a carmine spot at the anal angle. Posterior wing with a carmine spot on the inner margin and a spot of white below this.

Exp. $1\frac{9}{10}$ inch.

Near to *E. Inca* of Saunders, but at the same time abundantly distinct.

90. Erycina formosissima.

UPPERSIDE. *Male.*—Black. Both wings crossed near the middle by a broad band of white ending at the middle of the posterior wing : both crossed by a band of brilliant blue at a distance from the margin of the anterior wing near the margin of the posterior wing. Posterior wing with a short tail : three carmine spots near the anal angle, one of which touches the white band, the second the inner margin, the third below these and near it a small white spot : the outer margin spotted with white.

UNDERSIDE black. Anterior wing (with the exception of the margins and the band of white) brilliant blue. Posterior wing with a spot of white on the middle of the costal margin followed by a broad curved band of carmine which extends to the inner margin : the base and a spot on the tail brilliant blue : an anal spot and spots on the outer margin white.

Exp. 2 inches.

I cannot compare this to any other species ; beautiful as they are, this surpasses them all.

91. Charis victrix.

UPPERSIDE. *Male.*—Dark red-brown, with many indistinct spots of darker brown. Anterior wing with a subapical rufous spot marked with black and bordered on both sides with a line of silver. Posterior wing with the outer margin rufous, traversed by a series of black spots with lines of silver between them.

UNDERSIDE brilliant glossy blue, with the margins dark brown.

Exp. $1\frac{11}{20}$ inch.

Differs from *C. Regalis* of Butler in being of a brilliant blue below instead of on the upperside.

92. Emesis Cilix.

UPPERSIDE. *Male.*—Dark rufous-brown. Both wings crossed at and beyond the middle by two bands of dark brown *distant* on the anterior wing.

UNDERSIDE rufous, with the transverse bands as above

and a submarginal series of very indistinct spots : both wings with several spots at the base and one at the end of the cell all dark brown. Anterior wing with the central band at *a right angle with the costal margin,* angular in two places and near to the end of the cell.

Exp. $1\frac{6}{10}$ inch.

Anterior wings much pointed. Like other species, but may, I think, be known by the description which I have given of the underside. I have it also from Mexico.

93. Symmachia Titiana.

UPPERSIDE. *Male.*—Orange. Anterior wing with the base, the costal margin, a band from the costal margin before the middle to the inner margin near the anal angle, a short band at the end of the cell, the apex and outer margin all black: a pale yellow spot from the middle of the costal margin. Posterior wing with the apex, three submarginal black spots, the anal angle, and outer margin black.

UNDERSIDE as above, except that the costal margin of the posterior wing is dark brown.

Exp. $1\frac{3}{20}$ inch.

Unlike any other species.

94. Symmachia Asclepia.

UPPERSIDE. *Male.*—Orange, paler towards the margins. Both wings with a submarginal series of brown spots. Anterior wing with several indistinctly marked brown spots : three or four near the base, six or seven (linear spots) from the costal margin, and two near the middle of the outer margin. Posterior wing with two or three brown spots near the base.

UNDERSIDE as above, except that both wings are marked

throughout and on the outer margin with numerous brown spots.

Exp. 1 inch.

This species has the costal margin of the anterior wing slightly arched, not sinuated.

95. Symmachia Temesa.

UPPERSIDE. *Male.*—Brown. The costal margin of the anterior wing and the outer margin of both wings darker brown. Both wings with numerous dark brown spots, which it is easier to describe from the underside.

UNDERSIDE rufous: the margins brown, broad at the anal angle of the anterior wing and outer margin of the posterior wing. Both wings with three spots in the cell and spots above and below these: a spot at the end of the cell. Both crossed beyond this by three transverse bands (the middle band of the anterior wing imperfect) of black spots.

Exp. 1$\frac{1}{20}$ inch.

Form of *Symmachia*: colour of *Emesis*.

96. Lemonias Amphis.

UPPERSIDE. *Female.*—Orange. Anterior wing with the apex broadly brown, marked by two transverse bands, each of three white spots. Posterior wing with a bifid spot on the apex, two small spots towards the anal angle, the outer margin, and the fringe brown.

UNDERSIDE as above, except that it is paler: that the brown at the apex of the anterior wing is broken into spots on its lower border: that the apex of the posterior wing is marked by two black spots, which, together with those near the anal angle, are crowned with white.

Exp. 1$\frac{2}{10}$ inch.

Like the female of *Parthaon* (*Ancile*, Hew.)

97. Lemonias Amasis.

UPPERSIDE. *Female.*—Grey-brown near the base, dark brown at the outer margins. Both wings crossed beyond the middle by a broad common band of white. Anterior wing with five subbasal dark brown spots: posterior wing with two, all bordered on both sides with lilac.

UNDERSIDE as above, except that the posterior wing has seven spots near the base.

Exp. $1\frac{6}{10}$ inch.

Nearest to females of *L. Aristus.*

98. Lemonias densemaculata.

UPPERSIDE. *Male.*—Grey-brown, crowded with large dark brown spots and bands. Both wings with two spots in the cell, two spots below these (above also on the posterior wing), and a spot at the end of the cell all bordered on both sides with yellow: an irregular band of spots beyond the middle bordered inwardly with yellow, and a submarginal band bordered on both sides with yellow.

UNDERSIDE as above, except that the submarginal band is broken into spots.

Exp. $1\frac{3}{20}$ inch.

Nearest to *L. Balista* of Hewitson.

99. Lemonias Luceres.

UPPERSIDE. *Male.*—Orange-carmine. Anterior wing with the costal margin, the apex (where it occupies nearly one-third of the wing, is marked by a white spot and has its inner border nearly straight), and the outer margin (which is narrow) black. Posterior wing with the apex black.

UNDERSIDE as above, except that it is orange-yellow, and has the subapical white spot larger.

Exp. $1\frac{15}{20}$ inch.

Size of *L. cruentata* of Butler : a copy almost (but on an enlarged scale) of *Mesene Nola* of Herrich-Schäffer.

100. Esthemopsis Colaxes.

UPPERSIDE. *Male.*—Blue-black : the nervures broad and black. Anterior wing crossed by two semitransparent bands of white, the first of which commences at the base, fills the lower half of the cell, is divided into three parts by the median nervure and its first branch, and terminates not far from the anal angle : the second band towards the apex is regular and divided into four parts. Posterior wing semitransparent white, with the margins and nervures broadly black.

Exp. $1\frac{9}{10}$ inch.

Size and form of *E. Clonia* of Felder. Very nearly allied to *E. sericina* of Bates, but of different form.

101. Chamælimnas Phœnias.

UPPERSIDE. *Male.*—Dark brown. Anterior wing with a small triangular spot from the base, and a broad oval band (at a short distance from both the margins) brilliant yellow. Posterior wing with the costal margin broadly yellow from the base to beyond its middle, marked by a black spot at the end of the cell.

UNDERSIDE as above.

Exp. $1\frac{7}{20}$ inch.

Nearest to *C. Briola* of Bates.

———

Unwilling always to create new genera, I have felt it

necessary to make the four which follow. I have not done so, however, (not content with my own knowledge on the subject) without having the best advice. As to the position of *Threnodes,* which unfortunately has no antennæ, I had so much doubt that I hesitated to place it in this family until I had obtained the opinion of Professor Westwood. Mr. Bates (who has studied this group at home and in their native wilds) has kindly examined the species constituting the genera *Imelda* and *Lucilla,* and confirms the opinion I had formed, that they cannot be associated with any of the known genera, in all of which they would appear quite out of place. With regard to *Compsoteria* I have no doubt.

LUCILLA, *Hewitson.*

Head rather large. Eyes smooth. Palpi short, not visible from above, tomentose. Antennæ longer than half the wing, slightly thicker towards the point, spotless. Abdomen little more than half the length of the posterior wing. Anterior wing with the costal and outer margins and apex slightly convex : the costal nervure half as long as the wing, the subcostal nervure with three branches—two before (one very near) the end of the cell, the third branch halfway between the end of the cell and the apex : the cell broad, nearly half the length of the wing : the first discocellular obsolete, the second and third of nearly equal length joining the median nervure immediately after its second branch : the first discoidal nervure emitted from the subcostal a little beyond the cell, the second from the middle of the cell. Posterior wing regularly convex : the cell little more than one-third the length of the wing : the first discocellular leaves the subcostal immediately below its branch, the second joins the median close after its second branch : the discoidal emitted before the middle of the end of the cell.

102. Lucilla Camissa.

UPPERSIDE. *Male.*—Black. Anterior wing with a broad

oval orange band at the middle. Posterior wing cerulean blue with the nervures, the costal margin and apex (which are broad), and the outer margin black.

UNDERSIDE green-blue: the nervures broad and black. Anterior wing as above, except that the apex is green-blue.

Exp. $1\frac{6}{10}$ inch.

Very easily known by its remarkable resemblance to *Catagramma Tolima*.

IMELDA, *Hewitson*.

Head small. Eyes smooth. Palpi short, not visible from above. Antennæ half the length of the wing, with white rings, distinctly clubbed, the club long. Abdomen two-thirds as long as the posterior wing. Anterior wing with the costal margin nearly straight, the apex acute, the outer margin slightly convex: the costal nervure half as long as the wing: the subcostal nervure with three branches—two before the end of the cell, the third at a distance from the apex, the three branches nearly equidistant: the cell broad, half as long as the wing: the first discoidal nervure emitted at the end of the cell, the second a little before the middle of the cell. Posterior wing small, rounded: the cell half as long as the wing: the discocellular joining the median some distance above its second branch: the discoidal nervure emitted before the middle of the cell.

103. Imelda Glaucosmia.

UPPERSIDE. *Male.*—Brilliant glossy dark blue, slightly tinted with green. Both wings crossed beyond the middle by a narrow linear black band scarcely visible on the anterior wing: both with a submarginal band and the outer margin (which is broad) black. Anterior wing with the costal margin brown: crossed by a subapical broad band of white bordered with black.

UNDERSIDE as above, except that it is grey-brown, that

each wing has two small subbasal spots and a linear spot at
the end of the cell of dark brown, and that the inner band
is much broader.

Exp. 1$\frac{5}{20}$ inch.

Unlike any other species.

COMPSOTERIA.

Head small. Eyes smooth. Palpi long and slender,
smooth, the terminal joint rather short. Antennæ slender,
slightly thicker towards the point, half the length of the wing,
spotted with white. Abdomen as long as the wing. Anterior wing with the costal margin nearly straight, rounded
towards the apex: the outer margin rounded at the middle:
the costal nervure half as long as the wing: the subcostal
nervure with four* equidistant branches, two before the
end of the cell. The cell half the length of the wing, closed
by the discocellular nervures by an inward curve: the first
nervure short, the second and third of equal length, and
joining the median after its second branch. Posterior wing
short with the apex at an acute angle but rounded, the outer
margin slightly curved : the cell short : the first discocellular
nervure short : the discoidal nervure emitted near to the
subcostal.

104. Compsoteria Cascella.

UPPERSIDE. *Male.*—Transparent lilac-white: all the
margins and the nervures (which are broad) brown. Anterior wing with the cell crossed at the middle by a black line :
the apex (which is dark brown and covers nearly half the
wing) is crossed by a broad band of orange, marked by two
small transparent spots.

* This is without counting the termination of the subcostal nervure
(as some do), which ought to be considered a fifth branch if we are to
count a third median nervule.

UNDERSIDE as above, except that the costal margin of the posterior wing is marked at its base by three spots of white, and at its apex by a spot of orange.

Exp. 1$\frac{6}{10}$ inch.

In general appearance like *Ithomiopsis Corena* of Felder. I have a second species of this genus from French Guiana.

THRENODES.

Head small, eyes smooth. Palpi shorter than the head, pilose. Antennæ absent. Abdomen robust, one-third shorter than the wing.

Anterior wing with the costal margin nearly straight, curved towards the apex, which, with the outer margin, is much rounded, almost semicircular : the costal nervure two-thirds the length of the wing : the subcostal nervure with three equidistant branches, the first before the cell, the third near the apex : the cell half as long as the wing, closed obliquely by the second and third discocellular : the first discoidal nervure emitted from the subcostal at the end of the cell, the second near it. Posterior wing rounded : the cell very short, closed obliquely : the discoidal nervure emitted near to the subcostal.

105. Threnodes Cœnoides.

UPPERSIDE semitransparent grey-white, finely striated throughout with darker colour : the margins broad and black : the nervures black. Anterior wing with the outer margin very broad traversed by a series of eight large white spots. Posterior wing with the outer margin very broad : the costal margin marked below the middle by a small transparent spot.

UNDERSIDE as above, except that there is a spot of white at the base of the posterior wing.

Exp. 2$\frac{5}{20}$ inches.

Much like *Ithomia Cœno*, female.

LYCÆNIDÆ.

In the genus *Lycæna* there is one species only. In *Thecla* there are several, interesting chiefly from their dissimilarity to any that we know. Of these, I now describe 16 that are new, and am sorry that I cannot aid the descriptions by comparison with known species. There is one specimen, a female, of the beautiful and very rare *T. coronata*, one also of *T. Tuneta.*

106. Thecla Timoclea.

UPPERSIDE. *Male.*—Violet-blue. Anterior wing with an oblong brown discal spot within the cell, the costal and outer margins and apex very broadly dark brown. Posterior wing with two tails: the apex and outer margin dark brown: the lobe large, marked by a red spot.

UNDERSIDE dark brown, paler towards the outer margins. Both wings crossed by two submarginal bands of dark brown. Anterior wing with the dark brown of the base bounded by a line of darker colour beyond the middle. Posterior wing with a spot near the base and three spots beyond the middle towards the apex blue: a linear spot near the middle of the costal margin and some indistinct lines across the middle of the wing white: a black spot crowned with red: a minute spot of white above the lobe, and above it a linear red spot.

Exp. $1\frac{7}{10}$ inch.

Size of *T. Atys* of Cramer, but unlike any other species.

107. Thecla Atymna.

UPPERSIDE rufous-orange: the base brown. Anterior wing with the costal and outer margins and apex brown. Posterior wing elongated to its one tail at the anal angle.

UNDERSIDE rufous irrorated throughout with paler

colour : both wings crossed at the middle by a rufous-brown band bordered outwardly with paler colour. Both wings with a submarginal band of the same colour. Anterior wing with a linear spot at the end of the cell.

Exp. 1 inch.

Same form and similarly marked on the underside as *T. Loxurina* of Felder.

108. Thecla elongata.

UPPERSIDE. *Male.*—Dark brown : the fringe rufous. Anterior wing green from the base to the middle, below the median nervure : the discal spot (which is near the base) irrorated with white. Posterior wing elongated towards the anal angle, green from the base and abdominal margin to the middle of the wing.

UNDERSIDE dark brown, with the fringe white. Anterior wing with a linear spot at the end of the cell, two broad submarginal bands touching a little below the apex each traversed by a band of brown, white. Posterior wing undulated from a little below the base by white and rufous scales : crossed by a submarginal band of white traversed by a band of brown : the outer margin black bordered inwardly by white.

Exp. $1\frac{5}{20}$ inch.

Form of *T. Dinus*; unlike any other species in the colouring of the underside.

109. Thecla Theia.

UPPERSIDE green. Anterior wing with the costal and outer margins and apex broadly dark brown. Posterior wing with two tails : the apex and outer margin broadly brown.

UNDERSIDE grey. Both wings crossed (obliquely on the posterior wing) by four bands of brown, the fourth band submarginal (pale on the anterior wing): both with a pale brown band between the second and third bands : both with the outer margin and fringe brown. Posterior wing with the first two bands commencing on the costal margin near the base : the second ending near the anal angle in a short zigzag : a linear band between them closing the cell : a trifid band of orange above the tails.

Exp. $1\frac{5}{20}$ inch.

Unlike any other species.

110. Thecla Gaina.

UPPERSIDE dull pale blue. Anterior wing with the costal and outer margins and apex broadly brown. Posterior wing with two tails: the outer margin brown marked by two darker spots near the tails.

UNDERSIDE rufous. Both wings crossed by a band of white straight and beyond the middle of the anterior wing, commencing at the middle of the costal margin of the posterior wing straight until it forms the W of the posterior wing. Anterior wing crossed by a submarginal band of brown bordered on both sides with white. Posterior wing *crossed by a broad* submarginal *band of scarlet,* bordered above first with black and then with white, and below with white, marked between the tails by a black spot : the margin black bordered inwardly with white.

Exp. 1 inch.

Unlike any other species.

111. Thecla Epopea.

UPPERSIDE pale blue. Anterior wing with the costal and outer margins and apex (which is pointed) broadly dark brown. Posterior wing with two tails : the outer margin dark brown, very narrow.

UNDERSIDE rufous-grey. Both wings crossed by two linear bands of white: the first band at the middle, commencing at the middle of the costal margin of the posterior wing, and forming a distinct W: the second band macular, broken on the posterior wing: both wings with a submarginal band of white spots indistinct on the anterior wing. Posterior wing with a large scarlet spot between the tails marked by a black spot: a lunular brown spot near the anal angle bordered with white, and above it with scarlet: the margin brown bordered inwardly with white.

Exp. $1\frac{1}{10}$ inch.

I cannot compare this and the preceding to any species which I have yet figured: the band of the posterior wing is more obliquely placed.

112. Thecla Cleocha.

UPPERSIDE cerulean blue. Anterior wing with the costal margin, the apex, and outer margin (which are very broad) brown. Posterior wing with two tails: a submarginal band of brown broken into spots near the tails: the margin black bordered with white above the tails.

UNDERSIDE drab or stone-colour. Both wings with a white line at the end of the cell: both crossed beyond the middle by a band of white its inner border first white then rufous: straight on the posterior wing to the W which is very distinct: both crossed near the outer margin by a band of brown bordered on both sides with white: both with a submarginal brown band. Posterior wing with the lobe black, crowned with white, bordered outwardly with scarlet: a scarlet spot between the tails marked with black.

Exp. $\frac{19}{20}$ inch.

113. Thecla Gabatha.

UPPERSIDE. Anterior wing dark brown: the inner

margin from the base to near the outer margin and to the median nervure and its first branch, brilliant pale blue. Posterior wing with two tails: brilliant pale blue, with the costal and outer margins brown: two black lunular spots at the base of the tails : the lobe orange crowned with white : the outer margin black bordered inwardly with white near the tails.

UNDERSIDE pale stone-colour: both wings crossed by a band of white, bordered inwardly with brown, ending at the first median nervure of the anterior wing, below which there is *a sagittiform spot*: broken on the posterior wing into four parts before it forms the W : both wings crossed near the margin by a band of brown bordered on both sides with white. Posterior wing with a scarlet spot between the tails marked with black : the lobe and a spot near it black crowned with scarlet: the outer margin black, bordered inwardly with white.

Exp. 1½ inch.

114. Thecla Trebonia.

UPPERSIDE. *Male.*—Pale blue, tinted with green. Anterior wing with a large round discal spot within the end of the cell: the costal and outer margins and the apex beyond (touching the discal spot) black. Posterior wing with one tail: the outer margin black, narrow.

UNDERSIDE grey. Both wings crossed beyond the middle by a white linear band ending at the first median nervule of the anterior wing, forming a large and distinct W on the posterior wing : both crossed by a submarginal band of white bordered outwardly with darker colour and again with white. Anterior wing white and polished where it meets the lower wing, except below the shoulder, where it is black. Posterior wing with the shoulder much projected : the lobe and a small spot above the tail black bordered above with scarlet :

the margin brown, bordered above with white : the fringe white.

Exp. $1\frac{4}{10}$ inch.

Nearly allied to *T. Acameda* of Hewitson, from which it differs chiefly in having a discal spot.

115. Thecla Carteia.

UPPERSIDE. *Male.*—Brilliant morpho-blue. Anterior wing with the costal margin, the apex (which is broad), and the outer margin to the submedian nervure black. Posterior wing with two tails : brown and polished where the wings meet : the fringe dark brown.

UNDERSIDE drab or stone-colour. Both wings crossed beyond the middle by a band of white, bordered inwardly with rufous-brown : undulated on the anterior wing, very irregular and broken into spots on the posterior wing. Anterior wing paler where the wings meet, brown under the projecting shoulder of the posterior wing. Posterior wing with a submarginal zigzag band of brown, bordered on both sides with white : the lobe and a spot between the tails black, bordered above with scarlet : the outer margin brown, bordered inwardly with white.

Exp. $1\frac{9}{20}$ inch.

Near to *T. Ambrax*, but without the discal spot.

116. Thecla Cordelia.

UPPERSIDE dark brown. Anterior wing with part of the base towards the inner margin dull blue. Posterior wing with two tails : dull blue, with all the margins broadly dark brown.

UNDERSIDE stone-colour. Both wings crossed beyond the middle by two undefined bands of white. Anterior wing crossed beyond the middle by an undulated band of white. Posterior wing with a subbasal band of spots, two lines at the end of the cell, and a band of isolated spots at the middle all white: the lobe (which is black) and a small black spot above the tails bordered above with orange: the margin rufous-brown bordered inwardly with white.

Exp. $1\frac{7}{20}$ inch.

Belongs to the group which contains *T. Lausus* of Cramer.

117. Thecla Thespia.

UPPERSIDE. *Male.*—Brilliant morpho-blue. Anterior wing dark brown, the apex pointed. Posterior wing with two tails: the fringe brown.

UNDERSIDE green, brown towards the outer margins. Both wings crossed beyond the middle by three linear bands of white nearly straight on the anterior wing: the first band of the posterior wing commencing on the costal margin by an isolated linear spot, the W very distinct, the third band much curved: the lobe, a large spot between the tails, and *a similar spot near the apex* each brick-red and marked by a black spot. Both wings with the margin black bordered inwardly with white.

Exp. $1\frac{5}{20}$ inch.

A very beautiful species, and unlike any other.

118. Thecla Beera.

UPPERSIDE. *Male.*—Violet-blue. Anterior wing with the apex (which is broad) and the costal and outer margins (which are narrow) black: the discal spot oval and dark brown. Posterior wing with two tails: the outer margin narrow, black.

UNDERSIDE drab or stone-colour. Anterior wing crossed beyond the middle by a very straight rufous-brown band bordered outwardly with white: a submarginal brown band.

Published March 10, 1870.

Posterior wing crossed beyond the middle by a rufous band
bordered outwardly first with black and then with white,
commencing on the costal margin by a detached spot, zigzag
near the inner margin : a spot at the lobe and a large spot
between the tails (marked by a black spot) scarlet : a white
band bordered outwardly with black between these spots and
the apex : the outer margin black bordered inwardly with
white.

Exp. $1\frac{1}{10}$ inch.

Nearly allied to *T. Temesa* of Hewitson, figs. 284, 285.

119. Thecla Bosora.

UPPERSIDE. *Male.*—Dull blue. Anterior wing with
the costal and outer margins and apex (which is rounded)
broadly brown : the *discal spot very large* and of a *brilliant
blue.* Posterior wing with the outer margin black, narrow,
bordered inwardly near the tails with white : the fringe
brown traversed by a white line.

UNDERSIDE olive-brown, darker towards the outer
margins, which are black bordered inwardly with white.
Anterior wing crossed beyond the middle by two linear bands
of white : the first band with a detached spot near the inner
margin : the anal angle white. Posterior wing crossed at
the middle by six detached linear white spots bordered
inwardly with black : crossed beyond the middle by a band
of seven lunular white spots : a large spot at the lobe (which
is black), a spot between the tails (marked by a black spot),
and a *spot near the apex* all scarlet and bordered above by
the lunular spots of the transverse band.

Exp. $1\frac{1}{10}$ inch.

Nearly like the last described on the underside.

120. Thecla Camissa.

UPPERSIDE. *Male.*—Ultramarine or French blue. Anterior wing with the cell and the inner half of the wing below the first median nervule from the base to the outer margin nearly, blue : the remainder of the wing dark brown irrorated with blue between the median nervules. Posterior wing with two tails : the costal margin (which is broad) and the outer margin (which is narrow) dark brown.

UNDERSIDE stone-colour tinted with green. Both wings crossed beyond the middle by a band of white bordered inwardly with black, commencing on the costal margin of the posterior wing by a detached spot and straight to the W which is large and distinct : the lobe black bordered with scarlet, a large scarlet spot between the tails marked with black, both bordered above with black and white : a series of brown spots bordered on both sides with white between these and the apex : the outer margin black bordered inwardly with white.

Exp. $1\frac{1}{10}$ inch.

This species belongs to a numerous group, of which *Beon* is one, which I hope to figure in Part V. of the *Lycænidæ*. On the underside they differ little.

121. Thecla Calesia.

UPPERSIDE dark brown : the basal half of both wings brilliant green-blue. Posterior wing with one tail, the lobe large and projecting.

UNDERSIDE rufous-brown. Anterior wing with a line at the end of the cell and a band of four linear spots beyond the middle pale blue : two triangular spots of white near the apex. Posterior wing with the base red-brown irrorated with pale blue, marked at the end of the cell by a blue line, projecting between the first and second branch of the median nervure and bordered with pale blue : a large triangular spot at the apex, two spots at the base of the tail, the lobe, and a large triangular spot above it (irrorated with pale blue) all red-brown: a white spot at the middle of the costal margin.

Exp. $1\frac{2}{10}$ inch.

Form of *T. Irus* : underside unlike any other species.

122. Thecla arria.

UPPERSIDE. Anterior wing brown, blue from the median nervure to the inner margin. Posterior wing blue, with the costal and outer margins brown : slightly pointed at the anal angle.

UNDERSIDE. Anterior wing *blue under the base of the posterior wing* : crossed beyond the middle by a twice-curved band of brown bordered outwardly with dull white: a submarginal brown band. Posterior wing brown from the base to the middle (marked at the end of the cell by a black line), where it is twice deeply sinuated : the outer half of the wing grey-white irrorated with brown, and crossed by a submarginal series of lunular brown spots.

Exp. $1\frac{1}{10}$ inch.

Form of *T. Irus*.

123. Thecla oxida.

UPPERSIDE brilliant lilac-blue, with the costal margin, the apex, and outer margin (which are very broad) brown. Posterior wing pointed at the anal angle, cerulean blue, with the apex and outer margin brown : the fringe broad brown traversed by a white line.

UNDERSIDE. Anterior wing rufous-grey, crossed beyond the middle by a regularly curved grey-white band bordered inwardly with brown, and beyond this by an undulated band of brown bordered inwardly with paler colour. Posterior wing brown from the base to the middle undulated with darker brown, and bordered by an indented dark brown line : the wing beyond grey, with a rufous tint and crossed by a submarginal and marginal band of brown.

Exp. $\frac{19}{20}$ inch.

Belongs, like the last, to the group which contains *T. Irus,* and differs from it chiefly in the form of the band of the anterior wing.

HESPERIDÆ.

In this family there are nearly one hundred species, some of them until now very rare. In the genus *Pyrrhopyga* I have described two new species, one of which, *P. spatiosa,* surpasses in size any of the known *Hesperidæ.* *P. Nurscia* of Swainson, hitherto unique in the Hope Museum, is abundant, as well as the beautiful *P. Zereda* (*Hygieia,* Felder), described by me from the collection of Mr. Bates, and the still more beautiful *P. pardalina* of the Felders. Amongst other notable species, I may mention *Oxynetra semihyalina* and *Hesperia vulpina,* both of the ' Novara.'

124. Pyrrhopyga spatiosa.

UPPERSIDE. Body covered with rufous hair. Abdomen dark brown, belted with grey-white. Wings blue-black. Anterior wing with a triangular rufous spot of hair at the base : marked by three transparent white spots : the first and largest at the middle tripartite, the second bipartite, the third subapical tripartite. Posterior wing rufous, with the costal and outer margins broadly black.

UNDERSIDE blue-black. Anterior wing with the three spots as above. Posterior wing with two minute red spots near the base.

Exp. 3 inches.

The largest known species, most like *Cometes* of Cramer.

125. Pyrrhopyga Aræthyrea.

UPPERSIDE blue-black. The forehead, palpi, and anus carmine : the fringe white. Posterior wing with the outer margin broadly lilac-white, divided by the nervures into pyramidal spots.

UNDERSIDE. Anterior wing as above, except that it is slightly irrorated with white near the middle of the outer margin. Posterior wing lilac-white, intersected by the nervures which are black : the base violet-blue to the middle of the wing nearly.

Exp. 2 inches.

Much like *P. Aziza* of Hewitson on the upperside. On the underside, whilst this species has the outer half of the posterior wing white, *Aziza* is white at the base.

126. Æthilla Epicra.

UPPERSIDE dark brown : the *fringe white*. Both wings crossed near the middle by two bands of darker colour.

UNDERSIDE. Anterior wing as above. Posterior wing with the outer margin grey towards the anal angle, with a short white band above it sinuated on its outer border.

Exp. $2\frac{2}{10}$ inches.

The outer margin of this species, like *Æthilla Eleusinia,* forms a slightly curved line from the apex of the anterior wing (which is acute) to the anal angle of the posterior wing.

127. Æthilla Echina.

UPPERSIDE dark brown : the *fringe brown*. Both wings crossed beyond the middle by two bands of paler colour : the inner band broken on the posterior wing.

UNDERSIDE. Anterior wing as above, except that there

is a small white apical and subapical spot. Posterior wing with the outer margin broadly grey, except at the apex: *a submarginal band of white* dentated on both sides, *and above this a short broader band also white* from the abdominal fold to the middle of the wing.

Exp. $2\frac{1}{10}$ inches.

Very nearly allied to the last.

128. Hesperia Theoclea.

UPPERSIDE rufous-brown. Anterior wing with the cell dark brown.

UNDERSIDE. Anterior wing dark brown, paler at the outer margin, where the nervures are irrorated with white. Posterior wing silver-white.

Exp. $1\frac{7}{10}$ inch.

Shape of *H. Tiacella* of Hewitson (Exot. But. f. 27). The antennæ are, like those of *H. Cynisca* of Swainson, unusually long.

129. Hesperia Hermesia.

UPPERSIDE dark brown. Anterior wing marked by five transparent spots: one semitransparent at the middle of the submedian nervure, the second within the cell, the third (the largest) below this, the fourth between these and the outer margin, and the fifth (trifid) before the apex.

UNDERSIDE dark brown. Anterior wing as above, except that the spot within the cell is extended to the costal margin, that the spot on the submedian nervure is larger, and that there is a pale spot at the apex. Posterior wing irrorated with white near the base: *crossed near the apex* from the costal margin to the middle of the outer margin *by a broad band of pale yellow.*

Exp. $1\frac{8}{10}$ inch.

Form, size, and general appearance of *H. Salius* of Cramer.

130. Hesperia Hermoda.

UPPERSIDE dark brown : the fringe rufous-white. Anterior wing with seven transparent white spots : two obliquely across the cell, two below these between the median nervules, and three before the apex. Posterior wing with four semi-transparent spots beyond the middle.

UNDERSIDE as above, except that the outer half of both wings is rufous, that the anterior wing has a large white spot near the anal angle, and that the posterior wing has a blue spot bordered with black within and near the end of the cell, and that there is a band of five pale blue spots (larger than above) beyond the middle.

Exp. $2\frac{2}{10}$ inches.

Size and general appearance of *H. Sergestus* of Cramer.

131. Hesperia Carmenta.

UPPERSIDE rufous-brown. Anterior wing paler from the middle to the outer margin, paler still (*almost white*) *between the branches from the subcostal nervure* : the nervures dark brown. Posterior wing paler at the apex.

UNDERSIDE. Anterior wing pale yellow with the base, the apex, the nervures, and lines between those near the apex dark brown. Posterior wing rufous at the base, grey-brown beyond : the nervures and lines between them dark brown.

Exp. 2 inches.

Unlike any other species.

132. Hesperia albofimbriata.

UPPERSIDE dark brown. Anterior wing marked by three minute transparent white spots : one between the second and third branches of the median nervure, the other two together before the apex : the fringe narrow, dull white. Posterior wing with *the fringe broad and white*.

UNDERSIDE as above, except that there are three minute pale blue spots beyond the middle of the posterior wing.

Exp. $1\frac{8}{10}$ inch.

The broad white fringe of the posterior wing forms a distinctive character for this species.

133. Hesperia variegata.

UPPERSIDE dark brown, with some of the spots of the underside slightly traced.

UNDERSIDE rufous-brown : a line touching the subcostal nervure from the base to the middle yellow : a spot on the middle of the costal margin, a subapical spot, and the outer margin from the middle to the anal angle orange-yellow : a band of three irregular spots of yellow from the middle of the inner margin towards the apex : a trifid spot near the apex, a spot near it, and a spot below it lilac. Posterior wing with three oblong spots near the base, a band of seven spots below the middle (the central spot linear), and three spots near the outer margin all lilac : two apical spots and the inner margin (which is broad) yellow.

Exp. $1\frac{19}{20}$ inch.

Most like *H. callineura* of Felder, but larger.

134. Hesperia Hesia.

UPPERSIDE dark brown. Anterior wing with the costal margin from the base to the middle and a similar band touching the submedian nervure (which terminates in a small triangular yellow spot) rufous : an oblique bifid band at the middle and a small subapical spot semitransparent pale yellow. Posterior wing rufous : with the margins brown : marked by an oblong spot of brighter colour near the costal margin towards the apex.

UNDERSIDE rufous : the nervures of paler colour. Anterior wing with the base dark brown. Posterior wing crossed towards the costal margin from the base to the outer margin by a straight band of yellow.

Exp. $1\frac{3}{20}$ inch.

Very much like *Isoteinon vittatus* of Felder.

135. Hesperia Boeta.

UPPERSIDE rufous orange with the outer margins brown. Anterior wing with the costal margin brown, narrow : marked near the middle by *an oblique black line* as in the males of other species.

UNDERSIDE. Anterior wing dark brown where the wings meet. Posterior wing green-yellow, crossed from the base to the outer margin by two broad bands of white : the fringe white traversed by a band of darker colour.

Exp. 1 inch.

Very like *H. lineola* on the upperside, but with the costal and outer margins straight, the apex acute. Like *Anciloxipha melaneura* of Felder on the underside.

136. Eudamus Cynapes.

UPPERSIDE dark brown, rufous on the posterior wing. Anterior wing crossed from the costal margin before its middle to near the anal angle by a broad central equal glossy transparent band of white divided by the nervures into five parts, and before the apex by a curved transparent band divided by the nervures into six spots, the last two spots minute and separate. Posterior wing elongated at the middle.

UNDERSIDE as above, except that both wings are irrorated with ochreous-yellow, especially near the base and inner margin of the posterior wing, that there is a yellow spot below the central band of the anterior wing, and a linear pale spot at the end of the cell of the posterior wing.

Exp. $2\frac{1}{10}$ inches.

The antennæ of this species are unusually short, and somewhat resemble those of *Pterogospidea*.

137. Eudamus Centrites.

UPPERSIDE dark rufous-brown. Anterior wing triangular : a spot in the cell and a band beyond the middle (broken at the median nervure) dark brown : three minute transparent white spots near the apex. Posterior wing elongated at the anal angle : crossed beyond the middle by a band of brown.

UNDERSIDE as above, except that the anterior wing is irrorated with ochreous-yellow towards the outer margin, and that the whole of the posterior wing is thus irrorated, except towards the anal angle, where it is altogether yellow.

Exp. $2\frac{3}{10}$ inches.

Near to *E. Anaphus* of Cramer.

138. Pterygospidea truncata.

UPPERSIDE pale grey-brown. Anterior wing with the costal margin convex, sinuated near the apex, which is acute : the outer margin truncated, protruded between the median nervules, sinuated near the anal angle : marked by several central transparent white spots : one (bifid) on the costal margin, one in the cell forming three sides of a square, five below these placed obliquely across the wing, two of them below the first branch of the median nervure, two (the largest) between these branches, and one (minute) towards the apex : two subapical spots, one trifid, the other and lowest spot minute : a broad submarginal band of dark brown near the apex and anal angle. Posterior wing with a white line near the base, followed by a broad band of brown, a brown spot and suffused band of brown at the middle, and linear brown spots at the apex and anal angle.

UNDERSIDE. Anterior wing as above, except that the base is pale blue. Posterior wing blue-white, with the outer margin pale brown.

Exp. 1½ inch.

More angular in form than any other species known to me.

139. Leucochitonea flavofasciata.

UPPERSIDE dark brown. Anterior wing crossed transversely before the middle by a band of orange-yellow.

UNDERSIDE. Both wings with the basal half white and yellow : clouded with brown on the anterior wing and including the transverse band, its border irregular on the posterior wing.

Exp. 1½ inch.

Unlike any other species.

140. Leucochitonea Thoria.

UPPERSIDE dark brown. Both wings crossed at the middle by a band of yellow-white, narrow at its commencement on the costal margin of the anterior wing, broadest at the middle of the posterior wing. Anterior wing with three or four indistinct spots between the white band and the outer margin.

UNDERSIDE. Anterior wing as above. Posterior wing grey-white from the base to the white band : a series of indistinct submarginal white spots.

Exp. 1³⁄₁₀ inch.

Very near to *L. unifasciata* of Felder, but differs from it in having the *club of the antennæ white*, the central band more angular where the wings meet, and in being without the subapical minute white spots.

141. Leucochitonea Thestia.

UPPERSIDE. *Male.*—Dark brown. Both wings crossed before the middle by an irregular broad band of white commencing on the costal margin of the anterior wing, and ending on the inner margin of the posterior wing, divided into six parts on the anterior wing : two above the subcostal nervure, one in the cell, the fourth triangular, projecting outwardly beyond the rest. Anterior wing crossed beyond the middle by two bands of very obscure spots.

UNDERSIDE as above, except that the band is broader, and that the base of both wings is irrorated with white.

Female like the male, except that the anterior wing is crossed above (instead of the white band) by a series of obscure grey spots, and that both wings on the underside are crossed by two bands (one submarginal) of spots more distinctly marked than on the male.

Exp. $1\frac{3}{10}$ inch.

Unlike any other species. The female, although dissimilar above, from the absence of the band on the upperside of the anterior wing, has it below.

142. Leucochitonea Laoma.

UPPERSIDE. Anterior wing brown : darker from the middle of the costal margin to the apex : a band of grey near the base : a large spot before the middle divided by the nervures and brown lines into eight parts : three above the subcostal nervure, and one (large and triangular) below the median nervure : a distinct spot and trifid band below these : an oblique band of six spots (except one, which is lilac-grey) from the triangular spot to near the apex, and a small spot on the costal margin all white : a broad submarginal band of grey marked by two brown spots. Posterior wing rufous-brown, with a large trifid white spot at the costal margin :

some indistinct submarginal spots of brown bordered on both sides with paler colour.

UNDERSIDE. Anterior wing with the basal half white. Posterior wing white with the base grey-blue : a spot at the end of the cell, a band at the middle, a submarginal band (as above), and the outer margin brown.

Exp. $1\frac{2}{10}$ inch.

Resembles most *L. Lacæna* of Hewitson, but is without the angular wings of that species.

Supplementary Species.

143. Euterpe Eurigania.

UPPERSIDE pale yellow. Anterior wing with the base, the costal margin, the apex (where it occupies half the wing and is crossed by two or three yellow spots) and the outer margin dark brown : the inner border of the brown sinuated four times where it meets the central yellow, which, together with black nervures, it divides into four parts, one of which is within the cell. Posterior wing with the outer margin (which is marked by a series of yellow triangular spots), the nervures near it and at the base dark brown.

UNDERSIDE rufous-brown. Anterior wing as above, except that there is a fourth minute spot in the subapical band, three large spots at the apex, and a marginal series of hastate spots all pale yellow. Posterior wing with the basal half yellow, divided by the nervures, a line in the cell, and a line near the submedian nervure into eleven or twelve parts : the base itself brown marked by four spots, three of which are linear : a series of hastate spots on the outer margin, and at the point of each a conical spot all yellow : two minute spots of the same colour above the anal angle.

Exp. $1\frac{8}{10}$ inch.

This species was given to me some years ago by Dr. Kaden, in whose collection it then stood, if my memory does not deceive me, under a manuscript name. His specimens are of a somewhat darker yellow, and have the outer margin of the posterior wing broader.

144. Pieris Philoma.

UPPERSIDE. *Male.*—Dark brown. Anterior wing with the base of the inner margin grey-blue : a large trifid spot before the middle (one part within the cell) and a bifid spot halfway between this and the apex white. Posterior wing grey-blue, with the outer margin very broadly brown.

UNDERSIDE. Anterior wing as above, except that the costal margin is yellow, and that the apex is silvery white intersected by black nervures. Posterior wing silver-white : the base yellow : the nervures and lines between them black.

Exp. $1\frac{7}{10}$ inch.

Very nearly allied to *P. cæsia*, but with the underside of *P. stamnata*.

145. Ithomia Lycora.

UPPERSIDE. *Male.*—Transparent white : the margins of both wings broadly dark brown : the nervures slender, black. Anterior wing with the spur at the end of the cell from the second discocellular nervure : two dull white apical spots. Posterior wing with the nervures as in *I. Inachia*.

UNDERSIDE as above, except that both wings have a sub-marginal series of white spots.

Exp. $1\frac{15}{20}$ inch.

The least of the *Cæno* group, and unlike them all in its neuration.

INDEX

OF SPECIES AND THEIR LOCALITIES.

Page
1. Papilio Lacydes ...... St. Ines.
2. Terias Ecuadora ...... Island of Puna.
3. Euterpe Anaitis ...... Rio Topo.
3. ——— Ctemene ...... Rio Ashpiyaco.
78. ——— *Eurigania* ... St. Ines.
4. Leptalis Larunda ... Pisagua.
5. ——— Lua .... Sarayaco.
5. ——— Idonia ...... Rio Topo.
6. ——— Lysis .... St. Ines.
6. ——— Lelex .... Rio Topo.
7. ——— Leonora...... Rio Topo.
7. ——— Lygdamis ... St. Ines.
8. ——— Teresa ...... Rio Topo.
79. *Pieris Philoma*......... Limon.
9. Heliconia Cythera ... Angus.
10. ——— Alithea ... Jorge.
10. ——— unimaculata. Canelos.
11. ——— Hierax ... Rio Topo.
11. Melinæa Mæonis...... Sarayaco.
12. Mechanitis Mantineus. Angus.
12. Athesis Acrisione...... Villano.
13. Ithomia Mamercus ... Sarayaco.
14. ——— Achæa ...... Canelos.
14. ——— Antonia...... Jorge.
15. ——— Æmilia ...... Sarayaco.
15. ——— Æthra ...... Curaray.
15. ——— Varina ...... St. Ines.
16. ——— Phagesia ... Villano.
17. ——— Alphesibœa . Mapoto.
17. ——— Ægineta ... Rio Verdi.
18. ——— Thabena ... Rio Verdi.
18. ——— Harbona ... Mapoto.
19. ——— Tabera ...... Mapoto.
19. ——— Epona ...... St. Ines.
20. ——— Antea......... Rio Topo.
20. ——— Cœnina ...... St. Ines.
21. ——— Ticida ...... St. Ines.
21. ——— Ticidella ... St. Ines.
21. ——— Lamia ...... Curaray.
22. ——— Mirza ...... St. Ines.
22. ——— Alissa ...... Rio Verdi.
79. ——— *Lycora* ...... Mapoto.
22. Eueides Acacetes...... Curaray.
23. Acræa albofasciata ... Rio Verdi.

Page
24. Eresia Ildica .... Aguano.
24. ——— Letitia .... St. Ines.
25. ——— Casiphia ...... Jorge.
25. ——— Elæa......... Rio Verdi.
26. ——— Sestia .... Jorge.
26. ——— Mylitta......... St. Ines.
27. ——— Neria .... Sarayaco.
27. ——— Tissa............ Mapoto.
28. ——— trimaculata ... Rio Verdi.
28. ——— Alceta .... Rio Verdi.
29. Callithea Buckleyi ... Rio Rotuno.
30. Agrias Beatifica ...... Sarayaco.
31. Paphia Vestina ...... St. Ines.
32. Morpho Phanodemus. Rio Rotuno.
32. NaropeNesope...... Curaray.
33. Pronophila Tena....... Pooyal.
33. ——— Pomponia Pishcourco.
34. ——— Porcia ... St. Ines.
34. ——— Alusana . Alusana.
35. ——— Panacea . Alusana.
35. Euptychia cœlica...... Chunia.
36. ——— albofasciata. St. Ines.
36. ——— Ashna ... Sarayaco.
37. ——— Tiessa...... Jorge.
38. Mesosemia Marsidia . Sarayaco.
38. ——— Marsena . Rio Topo.
49. ——— Ama ...... Rio Topo.
39. ——— Adida ... Rio Topo.
40. ——— Zorea...... Canelos.
40. ——— latifasciata. Canelos.
41. ——— Ahava ... Rio Topo.
41. ——— Zanoa ... Rio Rushino.
42. ——— Mehida ... Rio Ashpiyaco.
42. ——— Zikla ...... Canelos.
43. ——— Ozora...... Canelos.
43. ——— Loruhama. Canelos.
44. ——— Reba ...... Canelos.
45. Eurybia Jemima ...... Mapoto.
45. Cremna Calitra ...... St. Ines.
46. Eurygona Athena ... St. Ines.
46. ——— Bettina ... Angus.
46. ——— Effima ...... Villano.
47. ——— onorata ... Sarayaco.
47. ——— Issoria...... Sarayaco.

INDEX.

Page
48. Eurygona præclara ... Sarayaco.
48. Necyria Juturna ...... Rio Topo.
49. Erycina pulchra ...... Barrancas.
49. ——— formosa...... Ashpiyaco.
49. ——— formosissima. Ashpiyaco.
50. Charis victrix .... Sarayaco.
50. Emesis Cilix............ Sarayaco.
51. Symmachia Titiana ... Ashpiyaco.
51. ————— Asclepia . Curaray.
52. ————— Temesa... Curaray.
52. Lemonias Amphis ... Sarayaco.
53. ——— Amasis ... Canelos.
53. ——— densemaculata. Curaray.
53. ——— Luceres ... Sarayaco.
54. Esthemopsis Colaxes . Pisagua.
54. Chamælimnas Phœnias. Sarayaco.
55. Lucilla Camissa ...... Rio Pindo.
56. Imelda glaucosmia ... Ashpiyaco.
57. Compsoteria Cascella. Aguano.
58. Threnodes Cœnoides . Mapoto.
59. Thecla Timoclea ...... Ashpiyaco.
59. ——— Atymna ...... Riobamba.
60. ——— elongata ...... Sarayaco.
60. ——— Theia .... Curaray.
61. ——— Gaina .... Curaray.
61. ——— Epopea ...... Curaray.
62. ——— Cleocha ...... Curaray.
62. ——— Gabatha ...... Curaray.
63. ——— Trebonia ...... Curaray.

Page
64. Thecla Carteia......... Canelos.
64. ——— Cordelia ...... Curaray.
65. ——— Thespia ...... Curaray.
65. ——— Beera .... Curaray.
66. ——— Bosora .... Curaray.
66. ——— Camissa ...... Sarayaco.
67. ——— Calesia......... Curaray.
68. ——— arria .... Canelos.
68. ——— oxida .... Jorge.
69. Pyrrhopyga spatiosa . St. Ines.
70. ————— Aræthyrea Mapoto.
70. Æthilla Epicra ...... Rotuno.
70. ——— Echina ...... Rotuno.
71. Hesperia Theoclea ... Jorge.
71. ——— Hermesia... Sarayaco.
72. ——— Hermoda... Canelos.
72. ———Carmenta... Banos.
72. ———albofimbriata. Sarayaco.
73. ——— variegata ... Sarayaco.
73. ——— Hesia ...... St. Ines.
74. ——— Boeta ...... Guayaquil.
74. Eudamus Cynapes ... St. Ines.
75. ——— Centrites ... Canelos.
75. Pterygospidea truncata. Canelos.
76. Leucochitonea flavo-
      fasciata .... Sarayaco.
76. ————— Thoria. Sarayaco.
77. ————— Thestia. Sarayaco.
77. ————— Laoma. Jorge.

EQUATORIAL LEPIDOPTERA

COLLECTED BY Mr. BUCKLEY.

DESCRIBED BY
W. C. HEWITSON.

PART V

No index issued
for this part.

LONDON:

JOHN VAN VOORST, 1 PATERNOSTER ROW.

April 11, 1877.

It is now nearly eight years ago since Mr. Buckley brought home his celebrated collection of butterflies from Ecuador. Since then he has been wandering about Bolivia, and is now returned to his old productive quarters. Before starting again for Canelos he visited a new district which he calls Jima, " a long way in the interior towards Loja," where he collected more than two thousand butterflies, but, being unwilling to risk the whole, has selected from them and sent me those only which he believes to be rare or new. Amongst these I find thirty-five new species, five of which, *Lycænidæ* and *Hesperidæ*, I have left undescribed. One of the most remarkable things in the collection is the *Paphia falcata* described by Hopffer, which bears striking resemblance on the upperside to the blue-banded *Preponas*. The collection contains *Morpho Juturna* also.

Oatlands, April 1877.

PIERIDÆ.

In addition to two new species of *Leptalis* Mr. Buckley has succeeded in sending me two of the species already known which I most coveted—*L. Rhetes*, of remarkable form, now in the collection of Mr. Oberthur, and figured in the second volume of the 'Exotic Butterflies,' and *L. hypocista*, figured by Felder in the voyage of the 'Novara.' Felder figures the female largely suffused with yellow on the upperside. Mr. Buckley sends the male, which resembles *L. Medora* on the fore wing.

1. Leptalis Medorilla.

Upperside. *Male.*—Dark brown. Anterior wing with a large quinquefid yellow spot below the middle of the costal margin, and three separate and equidistant spots of the same colour near the apex. Posterior wing with the costal margin

Published April 11, 1877.

where it meets the upper wing dull orange-yellow, crossed below it by a straight band of five yellow spots.

UNDERSIDE steel-grey, clouded with brown, which is irrorated with yellow : the yellow spots and bands as above, but paler on the posterior wing.

Female like the male, except that the anterior wing has a small yellow spot between the first and second median nervules, that the large yellow spot is lengthened into a band, and that the posterior wing has a second short band of yellow from the base.

Exp. 2½ inches.

2. Leptalis Ela.

UPPERSIDE. *Male.*—Dark brown. Anterior wing crossed by three bands of pale yellow—one from the base to the middle of the wing, one beyond the middle oblique, the third near the apex : the inner margin also yellow. Posterior wing yellow : the costal margin grey-white, the outer margin (which has a short irrorated yellow band near the anal angle) dark brown.

UNDERSIDE yellow. Both wings with a submarginal series of white spots. Anterior wing as above, except that the inner margin is grey-white. Posterior wing with a band of dark brown parallel to the costal margin, the broad submarginal band traversed by a band of yellow, the black bands united at the apex.

Exp. $2\frac{5}{20}$ inches.

Very near to *L. Pintheus* (*Eumelia*), but of much greater expanse, the fore wing narrower and of different form.

HELICONIDÆ.

Amongst the *Heliconidæ* there are a few good species. The *Eutresis imitatrix* of Dr. Staudinger, the new *Athesis* which I have now described, and the rare *Heliconia Cassandra*. In *Ithomia* there are fifty species, and amongst them ten that are new: several of them which, though at once seen to be good species, yet, having nothing but their size and neuration by which to distinguish them from each other, are very difficult to characterize by description. I hope to figure them.

3. Athesis Oligyrtis.

UPPERSIDE. *Female* transparent white: the antennæ, nervures, and margins (except the basal half of the costal margin of the anterior wing which is rufous) black. Anterior wing with a band at the end of the cell and a shorter band near the apex black: an indistinct band between the discoidal nervures near the outer margin: the costal margin marked by three small white spots: the outer margin traversed by an indistinct rufous band. Posterior wing crossed from the outer margin near the apex to the first branch of the median nervure by a band of black.

UNDERSIDE as above, except that all the bands are rufous, and that there are two white spots near the apex of the anterior wing, and one near the apex of the posterior wing.

Exp. $2\frac{9}{10}$ inches.

Near to *A. Dercyllidas*, but abundantly distinct.

4. Ithomia melanoptera.

UPPERSIDE. *Female.*—Black: antennæ black: the cell of both wings transparent. Anterior wing with the costal margin rufous: a submarginal band of semitransparent indistinct bifid spots. Posterior wing with the inner margin near the base transparent.

UNDERSIDE as above, except that the anterior wing has the costal margin, which is broad, some rays below it, and a series of spots on the outer margin rufous, and that the posterior wing has a submarginal series of quadrate rufous spots.

Exp. $2\frac{7}{20}$ inches.

Near to *I. Selene*, and of the same neuration.

5. Ithomia inelegans.

UPPERSIDE. *Female.*—Transparent, tinted with lilac: the antennæ, the nervures, and margins, which are all broad, black. Anterior wing with the band at the end of the cell irregular, protruded to the left, the outer margin dentated inwardly at the nervures. Posterior wing with an undefined spot at the end of the cell: the outer margin very broad, dentated inwardly.

UNDERSIDE as above, except that all the margins are rufous, and that both wings have a submarginal series of bifid white spots.

Exp. 3 inches.

May be a variety of *I. Ægineta*. Has the neuration of *I. Makrena*.

6. Ithomia cruxifera.

UPPERSIDE. *Female.*—Transparent: antennæ black. Anterior wing rufescent: the costal margin and nervures rufous: the band at the end of the cell, which is cruciform, and the outer margin, which is dentated at the nervures and marked by two white spots, dark brown. Posterior wing with the nervures, a narrow band at the end of the cell, the costal margin, the outer margin (which is very broad between the second median nervule and the discoidal nervure and marked by two white spots) black.

Exp. $2\frac{4}{10}$ inches.

In general appearance most like *I. Theudelinda*, with the neuration of *I. Antea*.

7. Ithomia Larilla.

UPPERSIDE. *Male.*—Transparent, slightly rufous: the antennæ, the nervures, and margins black. Anterior wing with a short irregular black band at the end of the cell: the costal margin beyond it to the apex transparent: the outer margin dentated inwardly at the second and third median nervules. Posterior wing with a black band at the end of the cell: the outer margin broad, marked by two or three scarcely seen white spots, and dentated at the nervures.

UNDERSIDE as above, except that there are three white spots at the apex of the anterior wing, and a marginal series of six similar spots on the posterior wing.

Exp. $2\frac{6}{10}$ inches.

Neuration of *I. excelsa.*

8. Ithomia Perasippa.

UPPERSIDE. *Male.*—Transparent rufous-white: the antennæ and the nervures black: the outer margins brown, narrow. Anterior wing with the costal margin rufous: the discocellular nervures long, in a straight line, very oblique, tending inwards from a small yellow spot on the costal margin, the angle near the median nervure. Posterior wing rufous near the inner margin, with the angle of the discocellular nervure unusually prominent.

UNDERSIDE as above, except that all the margins are rufous.

Exp. $2\frac{17}{20}$ inches.

Most like *I. Lorica* in size and shape. Neuration of *I. Apuleia.*

9. Ithomia Scantilla.

UPPERSIDE. *Male.*—Transparent, slightly tinted with lilac : the antennæ, nervures, and margins (which are narrow) black.   Anterior wing with the discocellular nervures (which are long and oblique and slightly thickened) tending inwards from a rather long white spot on the costal margin.

UNDERSIDE as above, except that the margins are all rufous, and that the costal margin of the posterior wing is yellow at the base.

Female like the male, except that there is a distinct narrow band at the end of the cell, a large white spot beyond it, and a submarginal series of five less distinct white spots, and that the apex of each wing on the underside has a white spot.

Exp. $2\frac{5}{20}$ inches.

Neuration of *I. Apuleia.*   Contour of *I. Lorica,* and though almost a copy of the last, yet abundantly distinct.

10. Ithomia Sulmona.

UPPERSIDE. *Male.*—Transparent : antennæ black.   Anterior wing tinted with lilac, its base and the posterior wing tinted with orange, the margins black : the discocellular nervure slightly thickened, oblique, tending inwards from the costal margin where there is an indistinct white spot. Posterior wing with the nervures rufous, except towards the outer margin, where they are black.

UNDERSIDE as above, except that the margins are rufous, that each wing has a single white spot at the apex, and that the base of the posterior wing is yellow.

Exp. $2\frac{4}{10}$ inches.

Most like *I. Terasita,* but without its broad margins. Neuration of *I. Cotytto.*

11. Ithomia Suesa.

UPPERSIDE. *Male.*—Transparent rufous-white : apex of antennæ orange, the nervures and margins black. Anterior wing with the band at the end of the cell equal, slightly curved inwards : an oblong white spot on the costal margin. Posterior wing with the angle of the discocellular nervure short, and near the base of the discoidal nervure.

UNDERSIDE as above, except that the margins are rufous, that the anterior wing has two white spots at the apex, and that the posterior wing has a marginal series of white spots in pairs.

Exp. $2\frac{15}{20}$ inches.

In general aspect like *I. Zabina.* In neuration like *Cotytto.*

12. Ithomia Granica.

UPPERSIDE. *Male.*—Transparent, tinted with yellow, except towards the apex of the anterior wing, where it is slightly lilac. Anterior wing with the nervures and margins dark brown, except the costal margin and median nervure to its first branch, which are rufous. Posterior wing with nervures and margins dark brown, except the discocellular nervule, which is rufous, with the angle large and prominent.

UNDERSIDE as above, except that the margins are all rufous except the costal margin of the posterior wing, which is yellow from the base to the middle, and that each wing has two very indistinct white spots at the apex.

Female does not differ from the male except in its broader margins.

Exp. $2\frac{4}{10}$ inches.

Very much like *I. Apuleia,* but with the neuration of *Cotytto.*

13. Ithomia Mira.

UPPERSIDE. *Male.*—Transparent, slightly tinted with lilac, the nervures and margins black. Anterior wing with a triangular black band at the end of the cell, and following it a distinct well-defined band of bright yellow from the costal margin to the third median nervule.

UNDERSIDE as above, except that the margins are rufous, with the exception of the costal margin of the posterior wing, which is yellow.

Exp. $1\frac{8}{10}$ inch.

Neuration of *I. Selene.*

14. Ithomia Hara.

UPPERSIDE. *Female.*—Transparent, slightly tinted with lilac : the nervures and margins (which are broad) black. Anterior wing crossed at the end of the cell by a broad equal black band, followed on the costal margin by a small white spot, and below it and near the outer margin by very indistinct white spots.

UNDERSIDE as above, except that the margins are all rufous, that the anterior wing has three small white spots at the apex, and that the posterior wing has six in pairs.

Exp. $2\frac{5}{20}$ inches.

Neuration the same as the female of *I. Zerlina.*

I would have been very glad if I could have put this with a number of varieties of *I. Zerlina* which Mr. Buckley has sent me.

ACRÆIDÆ.

15. Acræa Ara.

UPPERSIDE dark brown, slightly tinted with green. Anterior wing palest from the base to the middle, where it is crossed by a curved band of five white spots, the lowest of which is at the anal angle. Posterior wing with the nervures and lines between them black.

UNDERSIDE ochreous-yellow: the base of the anterior wing tinted with lilac : the central band broad, not in spots, as above: the apex and the whole of the posterior wing with the nervures and lines between them black.

Exp. $2\frac{3}{20}$ inches.

Nearest to *A. Hylonome* and *A. albofasciata*.

NYMPHALIDÆ.

16. Argynnis Sunides.

UPPERSIDE dark brown, crossed by four bands of fulvous spots : the third band of both wings composed of oval spots, three of which are marked with black : the fourth band of the anterior wing is of hastate and lunular spots.

UNDERSIDE. Anterior wing fulvous-yellow : three bands in the cell, a zigzag transverse band before the middle, two spots, a submarginal undulate band, and a linear spot near the apex black : the apex and outer margin grey, clouded with brown. Posterior wing grey-white, clouded with brown : four spots near the base, three spots (two bordered above with white) between the median nervure and the inner margin, and a submarginal band dentate on its outer border, all dark brown.

Exp. $1\frac{7}{10}$ inch.

This belongs to the Chili group of *Argynnis*, and resembles *A. lathonioides* on its underside.

In the genus *Catagramma* there are two species only that are worth notice, the rare *C. Ceryx* and the one described below, which is singularly different from any hitherto known species.

17. Catagramma Hazarma.

UPPERSIDE dark brown. Anterior wing with a short linear band at the base, a broad equal band on the inner margin from the base of the median nervure to near the anal angle, and a large trifid spot near the apex all ultramarine blue : the fringe spotted with white. Posterior wing with a submarginal band of irrorate blue spots from the anal angle to the middle.

UNDERSIDE dark brown. Anterior wing with the base ochreous-yellow : the apex yellow, bordered on the outer margin by black, spotted with white : a white spot on the costal margin beyond the middle : the inner margin broadly grey-brown. Posterior wing rufous-yellow, crossed transversely at and below the middle by two linear nearly parallel black bands.

Exp. $1\frac{8}{10}$ inch.

SATYRIDÆ.

18. Pronophila Phanoclea.

UPPERSIDE dark-brown, rufous near the anal angle of the posterior wing.

UNDERSIDE. Anterior wing dark brown, with a short white band on the costal margin beyond its middle, the apex rufous. Posterior wing rufous, undulate with brown, crossed from the middle of the costal margin (where it is irrorated with white) by a forked band of paler colour, one branch of which proceeds to the anal angle, the other to the middle of the outer margin, which is of the same colour as the band : a submarginal series of four or five black spots, each marked by a white spot.

Exp. $2\frac{2}{10}$ inches.

Unlike any other species.

19. Pronophila Phintia.

UPPERSIDE dark rufous-brown. Anterior wing crossed by an irregular rufous curved band. Posterior wing crossed by an angular rufous band.

UNDERSIDE. Anterior wing as above, except that there is a small pale brown spot in the cell, and that the apex is broadly pale brown, undulate with black. Posterior wing crossed transversely before the middle by a straight band of white: after the middle by a broad angular band of pale brown, bordered with white on its inner margin, broadest and dentate near the apex, undulated with brown, and marked near the costal margin by an eye-like black spot, with its centre white: two similar spots, but smaller, between the band and the outer margin.

Exp. $1\frac{8}{10}$ inch.

Scarcely differs from *P. Parrhoebia* on the upperside.

20. Pronophila Praxia.

UPPERSIDE dark rufous-brown, the outer margins darkest, the fringe spotted with white. Anterior wing crossed at the middle (parallel to the outer margin) by an equal rufous band. Posterior wing with a short rufous band from the costal margin below its middle.

UNDERSIDE. Anterior wing as above, except that there is a small rufous spot at the middle of the cell, that the central band is white at its commencement on the costal margin and becomes much broader towards the inner margin, and that it is irrorated with white near the apex. Posterior wing dark brown, undulate throughout with white, and marked by a white spot at the middle of the costal margin.

Exp. $2\frac{2}{10}$ inches.

The butterfly which I have described below is unlike any thing in my collection.

I leave it to those who are more skilled in juxtaposition than I am to determine its nearest neighbours.

ZABIRNIA, n. g.

In size and shape somewhat like *Catagramma*. Head small. Eyes smooth. Palpi very long and slender, twice the length of the head, clothed with long hair. Antennæ not half the length of the fore wing, terminating in a rather long club.

Anterior wing with the costal margin slightly convex, the outer margin more so, the inner margin very straight. The costal nervure, which is considerably swollen at its base, extends beyond the middle of the costa; the subcostal nervure has four branches, two before the end of the cell and two soon after it. The cell is a little longer than half the wing, and closed by three discocellular nervures, the first of which is short, the second tends inwards to a point and is angular, as in *Pronophila* and *Ithomia*; the third joins the median nervure at the base of its third branch.

Posterior wing with its outer margin semicircular, the cell closed, not half the length of the wing.

21. Zabirnia Zigomala.

UPPERSIDE dark brown. Anterior wing with the basal half rufous-orange, the nervures black.

UNDERSIDE as above, except that it is of a paler brown: that the apical half of the anterior wing and the whole of the posterior wing have the nervures and lines between them black: that the anterior wing has two ochreous spots near the costal margin beyond its middle, and a round black spot between the first and second median nervules: and that the posterior wing is crossed beyond the middle, parallel to the outer margin, by an indistinct band of paler colour than the rest of the wing.

Exp. $2\frac{3}{20}$ inches.

ERYCINIDÆ.

Amongst the *Erycinidæ* there are several new species, as well as additional examples, of some of the choicest things which enriched the collection of 1869. Of the new things most worthy of notice there is a second species of *Threnodes*, which, like the first one, bears a remarkable resemblance to an *Ithomia* of the *Cœno* group. There is, too, a second species of *Lucilla*, but in form very different from *L. Camissa*.

Amongst those previously known there is a female of *Erycina formosissima*, and specimens of *Zeonia Xantippe*, which do not differ from it, except that they are twice as large. There is a single example of the beautiful *Mesene Margaretta*, once in the British Museum.

22. Mesosemia tenebricosa.

UPPERSIDE dark brown. Anterior wing with a black triguttate discal spot bordered by pale brown : crossed beyond the middle by a narrow band of white, which changes to pale brown as it reaches the anal angle. Posterior wing crossed beyond the middle by a band of pale brown.

UNDERSIDE as above, except that it is paler from the base to the bands, that the anterior wing has a curved rufous band bordered on both sides with black, and a brown spot between the discal spot and the inner margin, and that the posterior wing has a small biguttate discal spot, with between it and the base two bands of brown, and bordering the transverse band (which is here white) three undulate brown bands.

Exp. $1\frac{8}{10}$ inch.

23. Mesosemia bifasciata.

UPPERSIDE. *Male.*—Blue-black. Both wings crossed beyond the middle by two broad parallel bands of indigo-blue. Anterior wing with the usual black discal spot bordered with blue, and marked by three minute white spots.

UNDERSIDE dark brown. Anterior wing indigo-blue in the middle : the discal spot as above, with a short black band between it and the base, two black spots below it, and a longer band outside of it also black : crossed by a submarginal band of white. Posterior wing irrorate with white : a discal black spot marked by two minute white spots : crossed obliquely at the middle, from margin to margin, by a band of black : a very indistinct submarginal brown band.

Exp. $1\frac{7}{10}$ inch.

Most nearly allied to *M. Meeda* in the colouring of the upperside.

24. Erycina Sepyra.

UPPERSIDE blue-black. Both wings crossed from the costal margin of the anterior wing, a little below its middle, to the anal angle of the posterior wing by a common, equal, continuous band of dull scarlet-red.

UNDERSIDE dark blue. Anterior wing with a scarlet spot near the anal angle. Posterior wing with the basal half lilac-blue, the nervures which intersect it black.

Exp. $1\frac{5}{20}$ inch.

25. Lucilla Suberra.

UPPERSIDE. *Male.*—Dark brown. Anterior wing with a large cordate scarlet spot, covering nearly half of the wing, a little before the middle.

UNDERSIDE as above, except that it is grey-green, with the nervures black.

Female on both sides grey-green, with a larger round orange spot beyond the middle of the wing.

Exp. ♂ $1\frac{7}{20}$, ♀ $1\frac{1}{2}$ inch.

In form nearly like *Limnas*.

26. Symmachia Suevia.

BOTH SIDES. *Male.*—Orange. Anterior wing, with the costal margin, apex, and part of the outer margin broadly black, crossed on the costal margin by four bands, by four spots, and on the outer margin by six linear spots, all pale yellow, marked below the bands of the costal margin by four black spots. Posterior wing with some central spots: the apex and two submarginal rows of spots all black.

Exp. $1\frac{1}{20}$ inch.

Most nearly allied to *S. rubina*, but much more beautiful.

27. Charis Subota.

UPPERSIDE white. Both wings crossed by six bands of brown : the fourth and fifth bands broken into spots and united at the anal angle, the sixth or submarginal band traversed by a silvery blue line : the fringe white.

Exp. $1\frac{2}{10}$ inch.

28. Emesis sinuatus.

UPPERSIDE. Dark brown, marked by numerous black spots, and crossed below the middle by a common band of grey : the fringe white. Anterior wing with a grey spot at the apex.

UNDERSIDE as above, except that it is of a uniform grey-brown.

Exp. $1\frac{5}{20}$ inch.

In shape this species resembles *E. angularis,* but is not half the size. Like it, it is sinuated below the apex of the anterior wing, and angular at the middle of the posterior wing.

29. Metacharis Syloes.

UPPERSIDE. *Female.*—Green-brown, with numerous black spots from the base to the middle: the outer margin broadly rufous-brown, traversed by a series of black spots separated by silver lines.

UNDERSIDE as above, except that the submarginal black spots are bordered with orange at the apex of both wings.

Exp. $1\frac{8}{10}$ inch.

30. Threnodes Trochois.

UPPERSIDE. *Female.*—Semitransparent grey, with the nervures and the outer margins, which are broad, black. Anterior wing with a submarginal series of seven white spots. Posterior wing with the inner margin scarlet.

UNDERSIDE as above, except that the posterior wing is white, and has a white spot at the base.

Exp. $2\frac{2}{10}$ inches.

BOLIVIAN BUTTERFLIES

COLLECTED BY

MR. BUCKLEY.

DESCRIBED BY
W. C. HEWITSON.

LONDON:
JOHN VAN VOORST, 1 PATERNOSTER ROW.

November 1st, 1874.

DESCRIPTIONS OF

NEW SPECIES OF BUTTERFLIES

COLLECTED BY Mr. BUCKLEY

IN BOLIVIA.

Mr. Buckley's Collection, like the larger one which he brought me from Ecuador, from which I have now described 154 new species, is in the most perfect condition, and, like the former collection, contains not only numbers of new species, but many things of great rarity and beauty.

He has brought a fine series of the splendid *Morpho Godartii*, of both sexes, a specimen of which in the collection of Mr. Salvin first determined him to go out and seek it. He has also brought the rare *Morpho Aurora* of both sexes. He was disappointed at not seeing either *Agrias* or *Callithea*. The genera which have the largest number of representatives in the collection are *Ithomia* and *Pronophila*. Of these I have already described and figured the new species in Part 92 of the ' Exotic Butterflies,' and therefore only enter their names here.

Of the genus *Papilio* Mr. Buckley has brought the following rare species, one of which was not previously represented in my collection :—*P. Lenæus*, *P. Madyes*, and *P. Warscewiczii*.

The *Catagrammas* are a splendid group, and, besides the three new species, include a large series of *C. Hilara*, *C.*

Marona, Comnena, Chaseba, Calamis, and of the beautiful thing which Mr. Butler has figured as *Latona,* which is for me a variety of *Sorana*; the female of *Latona* is without the carmine at the base of the posterior wing.

Mr. Butler, in describing his *C. Latona* as a female, says : —" As most of the specimens of *C. Sorana* are females, it cannot belong to that species." I feel interested in this question, because I have stated that nearly all the many species of *Catagramma* are without their females. All the specimens of *C. Latona* in Mr. Buckley's collection which I have examined, agreeing with Mr. Butler's figure, are males. Two specimens only, which are without the carmine at the base of the posterior wing, are females. Every example of *C. Sorana* in my collection is a male. In the whole of my collection, including *Perisama* and *Callicore*, there are not five per cent. of females, and these are confined to a very few species.

In *Pronophila* there is a series of two rare species—one the *P. Venerata,* which Mr. Butler, in describing it, says, justly, is " one of the most remarkable butterflies that has come for years," the other *P. Prochyta.*

The collection is rich in *Erycinidæ,* and contains two species singularly different from any thing we have seen before. For two of these I have failed to find a place in any of the known genera, and have admitted two more with some doubt.

PIERIDÆ.

1. Euterpe Amastris.

UPPERSIDE dark brown, with the basal third of both wings white, tinted with green and grey as well on the posterior wing, the base itself dark brown : both wings crossed beyond the middle by a series of pale spots (very indistinct on the posterior wing).

UNDERSIDE. Anterior wing as above, except that there is a short band from the costal margin beyond the middle, a submarginal and a marginal series of pale yellow triangular spots. Posterior wing yellow, with the base dark brown, spotted with yellow : a large central dark brown triangular band, marked by a yellow spot in the cell, and radiating from it to the outer margin by a series of linear spots of the same colour : a series of pyramidal outline spots of black on the outer margin.

Exp. $2\frac{1}{10}$ inches.

2. Hesperocharis Agasicles.

UPPERSIDE brimstone-yellow. Anterior wing with a minute brown spot at the end of the cell : the apex pale brown. Posterior wing with the anal angle produced, acute.

UNDERSIDE as above, except that the apical angle of the anterior wing and the whole of the posterior wing are undulated with pale grey-brown.

Exp. $2\frac{7}{10}$ inches.

A remarkable species. The base of the posterior wing is so produced upwards in the form of a shoulder as to cover the base of the anterior wing.

3. Terias Atinas.

UPPERSIDE yellow, with the base brown. Anterior wing with the base of the costal margin irrorated with brown: a black spot (sometimes two) at the end of the cell, and three small brown spots on the costal margin near the apex. Posterior wing marked by four indistinct brown spots, two near the middle, and two towards the anal angle.

UNDERSIDE as above, except that both wings have a minute black spot at the end of each nervure on the outer margin, and that the posterior wing has, besides the four spots described above, which are here more distinct, a spot at the middle of the costal margin, two small spots below this, and a spot near the inner margin all rufous.

Exp. 1½ inch.

I hope that I am safe in introducing this as a new species in a genus which is a complete chaos of descriptions. In form it is like *T. Læta* of Boisduval.

HELICONIDÆ.

4. Tithorea Tagarma.

UPPERSIDE. *Female.*—Dark brown. The fringe of both wings spotted with white. Anterior wing with several white spots: a longitudinal rufous band from the base enclosing the median nervure: two spots on the costal margin before its middle, four central spots, and a submarginal band of six spots all white. Posterior wing rufous, crossed at the middle by an ill-defined broad band of white: the costal margin, which has a white spot, and the outer margin, which is broad, dark brown.

UNDERSIDE as above, except that both wings have a sub-marginal series of many white spots, that the anterior wing is rufous beyond the middle, and that the posterior wing has two white spots near the middle of the costal margin.

Exp. $3\frac{9}{20}$ inches.

Very near to *T. Irene*, but is readily known from it by the two white spots near the costal margin on the underside of the posterior wing.

The following species of *Ithomia* have been figured and described in the ' Exotic Butterflies : '—

5. Ithomia Cyrcilla.

6. Ithomia Cleomella.

7. Ithomia Torquatilla.

8. Ithomia Pupilla.

9. Ithomia Crinippa.

10. Ithomia Ellara.

ACRÆIDÆ.

11. Acræa Byzia.

UPPERSIDE. *Male.*—Dark brown. Anterior wing with the space above the costal nervure, the cell, two spots below it, and a broad hexafid band scarlet.

UNDERSIDE as above, except that the apex of the anterior wing and the whole of the posterior wing are ochreous, with the nervures and lines between them black.

Exp. $1\frac{7}{10}$ inch.

12. Acræa Corduba.

UPPERSIDE. *Male.*—Dark brown. Anterior wing with
the base (except the costal margin) and a broad curved
hexafid band beyond the middle scarlet: the nervures and
the middle of the anterior wing black.

UNDERSIDE as above, except that the apex of the anterior wing and the whole of the posterior wing have the nervures and lines between them black, and that the posterior
wing is crossed parallel to the outer margin by a broad
undefined band irrorated with white: the abdomen is red.

Exp. $2\frac{1}{10}$ inches.

Nearest to *A. Laverna*.

NYMPHALIDÆ.

13. Eresia Corybassa.

UPPERSIDE. *Male.*—Dark brown. Anterior wing with
the base brick-red: a large central hexafid pale yellow spot
indented at the costal margin by a black spot: two minute
white spots near the outer margin. Posterior wing brick-red,
with the nervures and the outer margin (which is broad, and
traversed by a series of minute white spots) black.

Exp. $2\frac{9}{20}$ inches.

14. Catagramma Cabirnia.

UPPERSIDE. *Male.*—Black. Anterior wing with a
longitudinal band from the base to the middle part of a
broad tripartite band, which running at a right angle with it
ends near the anal angle; a bifid spot beyond the middle of
the costal margin, and a subapical linear spot all green: the
fringe alternately black and white. Posterior wing with a
submarginal band of green: the fringe white.

UNDERSIDE. Anterior wing with the basal half carmine, followed by black, marked at the middle of the costal margin by a white and blue spot: the apex white to a linear band, grey beyond it. Posterior wing white, crossed before the middle by a linear band of black, at the middle by a series of five black spots, and beyond the middle by a zigzag linear band of the same colour: the costal margin and the end of each of the bands carmine.

Exp. $1\frac{17}{20}$ inch.

Nearly allied to *C. Euriclea.*

15. Catagramma Cotyora.

UPPERSIDE. *Male.*—Anterior wing black, with a longitudinal band from the base to the middle, a spot near the middle of the costal margin, and two spots at the anal angle, all green: a linear trifid band of grey near the apex. Posterior wing brown, with a submarginal macular band of green-grey.

UNDERSIDE. Anterior wing dark brown, with the base, a spot at the middle of the costal margin, and the apex, which is crossed by a very slender black line, all silver-white. Posterior wing silver-white, crossed before the middle by an irregular black line, and beyond the middle by a series of five black spots and a zigzag linear band of the same colour.

Exp. $1\frac{10}{20}$ inch.

16. Catagramma Clisithera.

UPPERSIDE. *Male.*—Blue-black. Anterior wing with a longitudinal band from the base to beyond the middle, a short band below this divided by the submedian nervure, and a transverse band of spots beyond the middle, all brilliant blue: a linear spot of grey near the apex. Posterior wing with four longitudinal bands of the same blue and a submarginal band of grey.

UNDERSIDE dark grey. Anterior wing from the base to beyond the middle carmine: the costal margin lilac, the apex grey, bounded inwardly with black, marked by one white and three blue spots: the outer margin and a submarginal linear band carmine: the fringe alternately black and white. Posterior wing crossed before the middle by an irregular linear band of carmine, and near the outer margin by a band of the same colour: the fringe white.

Exp. 1$\frac{9}{10}$ inch.

A very distinct species, but most nearly allied to *Patara*.

17. Heterochroa Coryneta.

UPPERSIDE. *Male.*—Dark brown. Both wings crossed from the third branch of the median nervure of the anterior wing to the anal angle of the posterior wing by a common broad white band, both with a submarginal band of black. Anterior wing with a large triangular quinquefid orange spot near the apex. Posterior wing with a broad submarginal band of black, and some linear grey spots at the anal angle.

UNDERSIDE with the central band as above: both wings with the outer margin rufous and the anal angle white, with the outer margin near it and a submarginal line which divides it into spots black. Anterior wing with the base grey, two rufous bands in the cell bordered with black: a large rufous and white spot beyond the middle. Posterior wing with the base and inner margin white, succeeded by a rufous band bordered on both sides with black: the central band bordered outwardly with black, followed by a rufous band and by a band of grey-brown.

Exp. 2 inches.

Nearest to *H. Gerona,* but very different from any known species.

18. Paphia Cratais.

UPPERSIDE. *Male.*—Scarlet. Anterior wing with a small linear black spot at the end of the cell: a large triangular spot of purple (enclosing a large scarlet spot) before the apex, and from it a narrow band to the submedian nervure: the outer margin dark brown. Posterior wing tailed, brick-red towards the outer margin: a small orange spot on the middle of the costal margin, a band below this, and a spot near the apex, brown.

UNDERSIDE rufous-brown, tinted with lilac, and undulated with dark brown. Both wings crossed at the middle by a red-brown broad band: both with a large triangular space of the same colour on the outer margins. Anterior wing crossed in the cell by a brown band. Posterior wing with a silvery white spot below the middle of the costal margin, and three similar spots at the middle of the wing: two small black and white spots between the tail and the anal angle.

Exp. $2\frac{4}{10}$ inches.

A specimen which corresponds in every other respect with that which I have just described is without the white spots of the underside.

19. Narope Anartes.

UPPERSIDE rufous, clouded with darker colour, the nervures paler. Anterior wing, with the apex and an indistinct submarginal band of dark brown. Posterior wing with the outer margin orange-rufous, bordered inwardly with rufous-brown.

UNDERSIDE rufous, undulated with brown. Anterior wing crossed from the apex to the middle of the inner margin by a band of dark brown : crossed from the costal margin to the said band by three broad bands of brown. Posterior wing crossed by three broad bands of dark brown, with paler colour between them, and by a submarginal undulated narrow band of black, crossed beyond the middle by a series of minute spots, some black, some white, and by a submarginal band of lilac-white : the inner margin tinted with lilac and undulated with white.

Exp. $2\frac{8}{10}$ inches.

SATYRIDÆ.

20. Hætera Ceryce.

UPPERSIDE. *Female.*—Anterior wing semitransparent rufous-brown, crossed by three indistinct short brown bands (two in the cell) and by a longer dark brown band below the middle : three minute subapical white spots. Posterior wing rufous, crossed beyond the middle by a band of brown : the outer margin broadly brown, traversed by five white spots, bordered with black.

UNDERSIDE pale rufous-brown, undulated with dark brown. Both wings crossed by three linear common bands of brown. Anterior wing with a minute black spot near the base, and three minute subapical white spots as above. Posterior wing with five submarginal white spots.

Exp. $3\frac{8}{10}$ inches.

Probably only a variety of *H. Hyceta.*

21. Corades tricordatus.

UPPERSIDE. *Male.*—Dark brown, paler towards the outer margins, which are darker brown and strongly dentated at the apex of the anterior wing and below the middle of the posterior wing. Anterior wing with a minute white spot on the costal margin below the middle. Posterior wing with a submarginal series of black spots.

UNDERSIDE. Anterior wing rufous-brown, undulated with ochreous white; the apex darker brown, undulated with pure white. Posterior wing dark brown, undulated with white: two spots on the costal margin, a spot in the cell, and two pyramidal spots below the middle (which are bordered above with black) all white: the margins and a submarginal band black.

Exp. $2\frac{7}{10}$ inches.

22. Corades Callipolis.

UPPERSIDE. *Male.*—Rufous-brown: the outer margins dark brown, dentated. Anterior wing with a band of paler colour beyond the middle, sinuated on its inner border. Posterior wing produced at the anal angle.

UNDERSIDE dark brown. Anterior wing with the base and a broad band beyond the middle connected with the costal margin by a narrow band all ochreous white: a white spot near the apex, undulated with brown. Posterior wing undulated with lilac white, crossed before the middle by a narrow band, and beyond the middle by a broad band, very irregular on its inner border, and traversed near its outer border by a series of black spots: both pale yellow: a white spot in the cell.

Exp. $2\frac{6}{10}$ inches.

This, and especially the last described, are remarkable species, and very different from any that we have seen before.

The species of *Pronophila,* of which the names only are given below, have been figured in the ' Exotic Butterflies :'—

23. **Pronophila Panthides.**

24. **Pronophila Pandates.**

25. **Pronophila Perisades.**

26. **Pronophila Pammenes.**

27. **Pronophila Pactyes.**

28. **Lymanopoda Insulsa.**

UPPERSIDE dark brown, rufous towards the outer margins.

UNDERSIDE dark brown, irrorated with grey towards the outer margins. Anterior wing with two small white spots near the outer margin and a submarginal zigzag black line. Posterior wing with one similar white spot near the anal angle.

Exp. $1\frac{3}{10}$ to $1\frac{13}{20}$ inch.

ERYCINIDÆ.

29. Erycina Mira.

UPPERSIDE. *Male.*—Black. Both wings crossed at the middle by a common narrow band of scarlet. Posterior wing with a broad band of scarlet from the middle of the outer margin to the anal angle.

UNDERSIDE brilliant blue. Both wings crossed by a common band of black. Posterior wing with the band of scarlet as above, and a small spot of the same colour near the anal angle.

Exp. $1\frac{9}{10}$ inch.

30. Erycina Miranda.

UPPERSIDE. *Male.*—Black. Anterior wing crossed at the middle, at a right angle nearly with the margins, by a broad band of scarlet. Posterior wing with a short tail: brilliant blue, with the base and outer margin and nervures black.

UNDERSIDE brilliant blue. Both wings with the margins and a band across the middle dark brown. A small white spot near the anal angle.

Exp. $1\frac{9}{10}$ inch.

Differs from *E. formosa*, to which it bears great resemblance, in the position of the scarlet band.

31. Eurygona Chirone.

UPPERSIDE. *Female.*—Anterior wing with the base pale rufous-brown, the centre white, the costal and outer margin broadly dark brown. Posterior wing pale rufous-brown.

UNDERSIDE silver-white. Both wings crossed at the middle by a common band of orange : both crossed beyond the middle by two bands of rufous spots : the fringe rufous.

Exp. $1\frac{7}{20}$ inch.

32. Eurygona Corduena.

UPPERSIDE. *Male.*—Dark brown. Anterior wing with the base blue. Posterior wing with the anal angle of the same colour.

UNDERSIDE silver-white. Both wings crossed by three equidistant rufous-brown bands : the outer margin rufous. Posterior wing orange near the outer margin, where it is marked by a black spot.

Female.—Rufous-brown. Anterior wing with a large central white spot : the apex and outer margin dark brown. Posterior wing with a small central white spot.

Exp. $1\frac{4}{10}$ inch.

33. Nymphidium Anthias.

UPPERSIDE yellow-white, with the outer margins dark brown, very broad. Anterior wing with the costal margin dark brown ; a small white spot near the costal margin beyond the middle, and a smaller white spot near the apex. Posterior wing with a line and two minute spots of white near the anal angle.

UNDERSIDE as above, except that the anterior wing is crossed by two bands of white spots, and that the posterior wing has a double series of smaller spots between the anal angle and the middle : a spot of brown on the inner margin.

Exp. $1\frac{1}{10}$ inch.

34. Nymphidium Ænetus.

UPPERSIDE. *Female.*—White, tinted with yellow : the margins dark brown. Anterior wing with a white spot at the apex. Posterior wing with a submarginal linear grey band.

UNDERSIDE as above, except that it is without the grey band of the posterior wing.

Exp. $1\frac{9}{20}$ inch.

35. Nymphidium Cyneas.

UPPERSIDE. *Female.*—Orange, with the margins broadly black. Anterior wing with the fringe of the apex white.

UNDERSIDE as above, but paler.

Exp. $1\frac{1}{10}$ inch.

36. Lemonias Curulis.

UPPERSIDE. *Male.*—Green-blue. Both wings crossed

by seven linear bands of black ; the outer margins also black. Anterior wing with indistinct bands of brown between the first and second and third black bands : the fourth band zigzag, the sixth marked by some black spots. Posterior wing with the fifth and sixth bands united at the middle.

UNDERSIDE as above, except that it is grey instead of blue.

Female like the male, except there is a subapical white spot on the anterior wing.

Exp. $1\frac{3}{10}$ inch.

37. Lemonias Antanitis.

UPPERSIDE. *Male.*—White. Anterior wing with the costal margin from its base to the middle, and the whole of the cell and beyond it, dark brown; the apex and outer margin to the submedian nervure also dark brown.

UNDERSIDE white. Both wings crossed before the middle by a pale brown band, commencing on the costal margin of the anterior wing by a large brown spot. Both wings crossed near the outer margin by a pale brown band : the margin and some spots near it of the same colour : the outer margin of the anterior wing (where brown above) grey.

Exp. $1\frac{13}{20}$ inch.

Very unlike any known species, and in form like *Pandemos*.

HERMATHENA, n. g.

Head large. Eyes smooth. Palpi long, nearly smooth, twice as long as the head, the terminal joint smooth. Antennæ half the length of the wing, slightly thickened towards the point, spotted with white. The abdomen half the length of the posterior wing. Anterior wing with the costal margin straight : the outer margin regularly curved outwards. Costal nervure half as long as the wing : subcostal nervure with four branches, two before the end of the cell, the third and fourth

equidistant.   The cell broad, not half the length of the wing,
closed by the discocellular nervures by an inward curve; the
first nervure obsolete, the second and third of equal length,
joining the median nervure below its second branch : the first
discoidal nervure emitted at the end of the cell, the second
at its middle.   Posterior wing with the outer margin circular,
the cell not half the length of the wing, closed obliquely.

38. Hermathena Candidata.

UPPERSIDE. *Female.*—White.   Both wings with marginal grey spots.   Anterior wing with a spot on the costal
margin at the end of the cell, and three large spots (one
apical) on the outer margin, all pale grey-brown.   Posterior
wing with four or five marginal spots, the apical spot larger
then the rest, which are minute.

UNDERSIDE as above, except that the marginal spots are
dark brown.

Exp. 1½ to 2 inches.

A remarkable species, differing much in size; the larger
specimens of the form and size of *Pandemos Arcas.*

39. Symmachia Chrysame.

UPPERSIDE. *Male.*—Brown.   Both wings irrorated with
gold-green from the base to beyond the middle, both crossed
beyond this by a band of lilac irrorated on the posterior with
gold, by a band of dark brown, by a band of rufous-brown,
by a band of gold-green bordered above with black, and by a
second rufous band bordered outwardly with black : the fringe
lilac and brown.

UNDERSIDE grey-brown.   Both wings with several spots
near the base : both crossed by two bands of dark brown at
and beyond the middle.   Anterior wing irrorated at the base
by gold-green and blue, and marked below the costal margin
from the base to the apex by several grey spots irrorated with

silver in a strong light. Posterior wing with a submarginal series of black spots.

Exp. 1 inch.

40. Bæotis Felix.

UPPERSIDE. *Male.*—White, tinted with pale yellow, chiefly near the base: the margins and a common band, which commences at the middle of the costal margin of the anterior wing, crosses the wings near the base, and ends at the anal angle of the posterior wing, brown. Anterior wing with a silver spot at the apex. Posterior with a submarginal band of the same colour.

UNDERSIDE as above, except that it is without the submarginal silver band.

Exp. $1\frac{5}{20}$ inch.

41. Bæotis Creusis.

UPPERSIDE black. Both wings crossed at the middle by a common band of white, broad in the middle, narrow at each end: both crossed beyond the middle by a band of silver, by a linear band of pale yellow, and by a submarginal band of silver.

UNDERSIDE dark brown. Both wings crossed by a band near the base, the central band as above, and a band much broader than above (broken where the wings meet) near the outer margin, all white: a very indistinct submarginal silver line.

Exp. $1\frac{2}{10}$ inch.

XYNIAS, n. g.

Head rather large. Eyes smooth. Palpi only half the length of the head, slightly covered with scales. Antennæ half as long as the wing, slender, slightly thicker towards the

point, spotless. Abdomen nearly as long as the posterior
wing.

Anterior wing slightly concave at the middle of the costal
margin, circular at the apex. The costal nervure half as long
as the wing: the subcostal nervure with three branches, two
of which are before the end of the cell, the third halfway
between the cell and the apex: the cell half the length of the
wing: the first discocellular nervure short, the second and
third of equal length, joining the median nervure at some
distance beyond its second branch, and closing the cell per-
pendicularly: the first discoidal nervure emitted at the end
of the cell. Posterior wing triangular, the outer margin,
which is straight, forming a right angle with the abdominal
margin; the cell half as long as the wing, closed at a right
angle.

42. Xynias Cynosema.

UPPERSIDE. *Male.*—Transparent lilac-white; the nervures black. Anterior wing with the costal margin and the
apical half, which is crossed by a broad band of white, dark
brown; the inner margin orange, bordered inwardly with
dark brown. Posterior wing with all the margins dark
brown.

UNDERSIDE exactly as above.

Exp. $2\frac{9}{20}$ inch.

Like the species of *Ithomiola*, but different in the neuration
of the wings.

43. Limnas Cercopes.

UPPERSIDE. *Male.*—Black. Anterior wing with a short
marginal band of orange near the anal angle. Posterior
wing with the outer margin, except at the apex, of the same
colour.

UNDERSIDE as above, except that the nervures are white,

and that there is a carmine spot at the base of the posterior wing.

Exp. $1\frac{6}{10}$ inch.

44. Limnas Ægates.

UPPERSIDE. *Male.*—Dark brown, with the nervures pale brown. Anterior wing with a scarlet spot at the base, a short band beyond the middle, and the apex white. Posterior wing with the fringe white.

UNDERSIDE as above, except that there are two scarlet spots at the base of the anterior wing, and one near that of the posterior wing. Anterior wing with a round white spot at the apex.

Exp. $1\frac{6}{10}$ inch.

45. Limnas Ambryllis.

UPPERSIDE. *Male.*—Black: the nervures paler. Anterior wing with a scarlet spot near the base; crossed beyond the middle by a narrow band of white divided into spots near the outer margin. Posterior wing with a submarginal band of white sometimes divided into spots.

UNDERSIDE as above, except that the nervures are paler, that the anterior wing has two scarlet spots near the base, and the posterior wing one spot of the same colour.

Exp. $1\frac{6}{10}$ to $1\frac{9}{10}$ inch.

LYCÆNIDÆ.

46. Thecla circinata.

UPPERSIDE blue. Anterior wing with the outer half dark brown. Posterior wing semicircular, tailless, with the costal margin and apex broadly brown.

UNDERSIDE. Anterior wing with a central spot of dark

brown: crossed beyond the middle by a linear band of white. Posterior wing crossed by two linear bands of white: the first before the middle, direct, broken into spots; the second beyond the middle, zigzag.

Exp. $1\frac{5}{20}$ inch.

A remarkable species, resembling in form *Pseudolycæna Platyptera* of Felder.

47. Thecla Crambusa.

UPPERSIDE dark brown, with the fringe white. Anterior wing sinuated below the apex and at the middle of the outer margin. Posterior wing with one tail: two black spots, bordered above with white, at the base of the tail, the lobe projecting like a tail.

UNDERSIDE. Anterior wing rufous, crossed beyond the middle by a dark brown band bordered outwardly with white; three brown spots below this band, and four on the outer margin. Posterior wing dark brown, with a large triangular white spot at the middle of the costal margin; several black spots between this and the inner margin bordered on both sides with white: the lobe, and three spots towards the apex, black, with, between them, some white spots.

Exp. 1 inch.

Belongs to the same group as *T. Thius*.

HESPERIDÆ.

48. Pyrrhopyga Cosinga.

UPPERSIDE dark green, with the fringe white. Both wings crossed beyond the middle by a series of rufous-orange spots. Anterior wing with a longitudinal spot within the cell, a similar spot between the median nervules, and three spots between it and the inner margin, all rufous-orange.

Posterior wing with a spot within the cell, and two small spots between it and the inner margin of the same colour: the palpi, head, thorax, and anus carmine.

UNDERSIDE as above, except that the spots and bands are larger and broader.

Exp. $2\frac{11}{20}$ inches.

49. Pyrrhopyga Phylleia.

UPPERSIDE dark brown, with the outer margins (broadest on the posterior wing), the palpi, head, neck, and anus carmine.

UNDERSIDE as above.

Exp. $2\frac{3}{10}$ inches.

Does not differ from *P. Hadassa*, except that it has no longitudinal carmine bands on the thorax.

50. Ericides Charonotis.

UPPERSIDE blue-black. Anterior wing with four spots from the base, one spot near the inner margin, one near the costal margin, beyond its middle, and a series of six spots near the outer margin, all irrorated with green; a trifid band at the middle, a bifid spot beyond this, a bifid spot and two minute spots near the apex, all pale yellow, transparent. Posterior wing with a band from the base to the middle of the wing, a band near the inner margin, a short band from the middle of the costal margin, and a series of eight spots parallel to the outer margin, all orange-yellow: the outer margin spotted with white, the thorax with a longitudinal band of yellow on each side, the abdomen with a series of spots of the same colour.

UNDERSIDE as above, except that the submarginal green spots of the anterior wing are orange.

Exp. $2\frac{6}{10}$ inches.

51. Eudamus Barisses.

UPPERSIDE rufous-brown : the fringe brown and white alternately. Anterior wing with a broad quadripartite band at the middle, a spot beyond this, and three spots near the apex, transparent, yellow.

UNDERSIDE. Anterior wing as above, except that there is a line of white between the single transparent spot and the spots near the apex, and a band of grey near the outer margin. Posterior wing dark brown, with the centre rufous : crossed before the middle by a broken band of silver, and beyond the middle by a narrow zigzag band of white, broader and silvery near the anal angle : a submarginal band of grey.

Exp. $2\frac{3}{10}$ inches.

52. Syrichtus Bocchoris.

UPPERSIDE dark brown, grey near the base : the fringe broad, black and white alternately. Anterior wing crossed by an oblique band of three spots before the middle, and beyond the middle by an irregular band of nine spots, all white. Posterior wing with a central white spot and a submarginal band of indistinct pale spots.

UNDERSIDE white. Anterior wing clouded with pale rufous-brown; the white spots as above, bordered with dark brown. Posterior wing tinted with grey towards the inner margin, and marked by several black spots—one at the base, two below this, three of unusual form before the middle, and a broken irregular band beyond the middle.

Exp. $1\frac{3}{20}$ inch.

Like most of the European species above, but altogether different below.